| Agriculture

Other Books in the Current Controversies Series

Agriculture

Lisa Idzikowski, Book Editor

GREENHAVEN
PUBLISHING

Published in 2021 by Greenhaven Publishing, LLC
353 3rd Avenue, Suite 255, New York, NY 10010

Articles in Greenhaven Publishing anthologies are often edited for length to meet page
requirements. In addition, original titles of these works are changed to clearly present
the main thesis and to explicitly indicate the author's opinion. Every effort is made to
ensure that Greenhaven Publishing accurately reflects the original intent of the authors.
Every effort has been made to trace the owners of the copyrighted material.

Cover image: Valentin Valkov/Shutterstock.com

Library of Congress Cataloging-in-Publication Data

Names: Idzikowski, Lisa, editor.
Title: Agriculture / Lisa Idzikowski, editor.
Description: First edition. | New York : Greenhaven Publishing, 2021. |
    Series: Current controversies | Includes bibliographical references and
    index. | Audience: Grades 9–12.
Identifiers: LCCN 2019057186 | ISBN 9781534506978 (library binding) | ISBN
    9781534506961 (paperback)
Subjects: LCSH: Agriculture History—United States. | Agricultural
    innovations—Environmental aspects. | Factory farms—United States.
Classification: LCC S441 .A356 2021 | DDC 630—dc23
LC record available at https://lccn.loc.gov/2019057186

Manufactured in the United States of America

Website: http://greenhavenpublishing.com

Contents

Chapter 1: Does the Global Agricultural System Meet and Secure Nutritional Needs?

Yes: The Global Agricultural System Provides for Nutritional Needs

No: The Global Agricultural System Fails to Meet and Secure Nutritional Needs

No matter how you look at it, the food produced today is not as healthy as it needs to be. In fact, agricultural practices are making it nearly impossible for much of the world's population to avoid negative health effects, and major changes must be made.

Chapter 2: Are Family Farms Obsolete?

Yes: Independent Family Farms Are No Longer Viable

community farming practiced by certain groups is a better and more successful alternative in today's agricultural industry.

No: Family Farms Still Have a Place in Agriculture

Black family farmers have played—and continue to play—an essential role in American agriculture but have often been subjected to discriminatory practices that make operating a farm even more difficult. As such, cooperatives and funding help farmers overcome these obstacles.

How can global hunger be eliminated? What can raise the economic standards in places mired in poverty? The answer to both these problems is to encourage and support family farming systems around the world.

This viewpoint compares family farms to industrial farms from a variety of perspectives. To the authors, it is clear that family farms are better than industrial farms from many different angles.

Chapter 3: Should There Be More Government Regulation and Intervention in Agriculture?

Agriculture, like other enterprises, is often affected by the economies of the countries involved. The question is when—and whether—a country's government should pass and enforce regulations to control agriculture.

Yes: More Government Regulation and Intervention Is Necessary

Some believe that GMOs need to be regulated. Are GMOs safe? Will their growth and consumption have unintended consequences? In some cases these answers are not currently known. Consumers want to have safe food, and some have sworn off GMOs to ensure this.

No: Government Regulation and Interference Harm the Agriculture Industry and Consumers

Chapter 4: Are Agricultural Practices Environmentally Sustainable?

Foreword

"Controversy" is a word that has an undeniably unpleasant connotation. It carries a definite negative charge. Controversy can spoil family gatherings, spread a chill around classroom and campus discussion, inflame public discourse, open raw civic wounds, and lead to the ouster of public officials. We often feel that controversy is almost akin to bad manners, a rude and shocking eruption of that which must not be spoken or thought of in polite, tightly guarded society. To avoid controversy, to quell controversy, is often seen as a public good, a victory for etiquette, perhaps even a moral or ethical imperative.

Yet the studious, deliberate avoidance of controversy is also a whitewashing, a denial, a death threat to democracy. It is a false sterilizing and sanitizing and superficial ordering of the messy, ragged, chaotic, at times ugly processes by which a healthy democracy identifies and confronts challenges, engages in passionate debate about appropriate approaches and solutions, and arrives at something like a consensus and a broadly accepted and supported way forward. Controversy is the megaphone, the speaker's corner, the public square through which the citizenry finds and uses its voice. Controversy is the life's blood of our democracy and absolutely essential to the vibrant health of our society.

Our present age is certainly no stranger to controversy. We are consumed by fierce debates about technology, privacy, political correctness, poverty, violence, crime and policing, guns, immigration, civil and human rights, terrorism, militarism, environmental protection, and gender and racial equality. Loudly competing voices are raised every day, shouting opposing opinions, putting forth competing agendas, and summoning starkly different visions of a utopian or dystopian future. Often these voices attempt to shout the others down; there is precious little listening and considering among the cacophonous din. Yet listening and considering, too, are essential to the health of a democracy. If controversy is democracy's lusty lifeblood, respectful listening and careful thought are its higher faculties, its brain, its conscience.

Current Controversies does not shy away from or attempt to hush the loudly competing voices. It seeks to provide readers with as wide and representative as possible a range of articulate voices on any given controversy of the day, separates each one out to allow it to be heard clearly and fairly, and encourages careful listening to each of these well-crafted, thoughtfully expressed opinions, supplied by some of today's leading academics, thinkers, analysts, politicians, policy makers, economists, activists, change agents, and advocates. Only after listening to a wide range of opinions on an issue, evaluating the strengths and weaknesses of each argument, assessing how well the facts and available evidence mesh with the stated opinions and conclusions, and thoughtfully and critically examining one's own beliefs and conscience can the reader begin to arrive at his or her own conclusions and articulate his or her own stance on the spotlighted controversy.

This process is facilitated and supported in each Current Controversies volume by an introduction and chapter overviews that provide readers with the essential context they need to begin engaging with the spotlighted controversies, with the debates surrounding them, and with their own perhaps shifting or nascent opinions on them. Chapters are organized around several key questions that are answered with diverse opinions representing all points on the political spectrum. In its content, organization, and methodology, readers are encouraged to determine the authors' point of view and purpose, interrogate and analyze the various arguments and their rhetoric and structure, evaluate the arguments' strengths and weaknesses, test their claims against available facts and evidence, judge the validity of the reasoning, and bring into clearer, sharper focus the reader's own beliefs and conclusions and how they may differ from or align with those in the collection or those of classmates.

Research has shown that reading comprehension skills improve dramatically when students are provided with compelling, intriguing, and relevant "discussable" texts. The subject matter of these collections could not be more compelling, intriguing, or urgently relevant to today's students and the world they are poised to inherit. The anthologized articles also provide the basis for stimulating, lively, and passionate classroom debates. Students who are compelled to anticipate objections to their own argument and identify the flaws in those of an opponent read more carefully, think more critically, and steep themselves in relevant context, facts, and information more thoroughly. In short, using discussable text of the kind provided by every single volume in the Current Controversies series encourages close reading, facilitates reading comprehension, fosters research, strengthens critical thinking, and greatly enlivens and energizes classroom discussion and participation. The entire learning process is deepened, extended, and strengthened.

If we are to foster a knowledgeable, responsible, active, and engaged citizenry, we must provide readers with the intellectual, interpretive, and critical-thinking tools and experience necessary to make sense of the world around them and of the all-important debates and arguments that inform it. We must encourage them not to run away from or attempt to quell controversy but to embrace it in a responsible, conscientious, and thoughtful way, to sharpen and strengthen their own informed opinions by listening to and critically analyzing those of others. This series encourages respectful engagement with and analysis of current controversies and competing opinions and fosters a resulting increase in the strength and rigor of one's own opinions and stances. As such, it helps readers assume their rightful place in the public square and provides them with the skills necessary to uphold their awesome responsibility—guaranteeing the continued and future health of a vital, vibrant, and free democracy.

Introduction

> *"Everyone has the right to a standard of living adequate for the health and well-being of himself and his family, including food."*
>
> —*Universal Declaration of Human Rights*

A griculture may bring to mind very different things to different people. Some might think of a ripening field of corn in August. Others imagine a herd of black-and-white dairy cows heading for the barn. Some might think of wide-open grasslands where domesticated animals graze in the fields. Others still might envision buckets of maple syrup fresh from the trees, or baskets of apples being picked in an autumn orchard. *Merriam-Webster* defines agriculture as "the science, art, or practice of cultivating the soil, producing crops, and raising livestock and in varying degrees the preparation and marketing of the resulting products,"[1] and a farmer as someone who "cultivates land or crops or raises animals (such as livestock or fish)."[2]

Naturally, people most likely equate agriculture with food, although many—maybe even most—people buy their food in grocery stores nowadays and consequently have no direct experience with agriculture. However, according to the US National Gardening Association, (NGA), there has been a large increase in the number of people who are interested in and actually growing food for themselves.[3] In fact, in the United States one in three households are now growing some of their own food. As found by the NGA:

The number of households participating in food gardening from 2008 to 2013 grew from 36 million households to 42 million households. That's an overall increase in participation of 17% in 5 years and a compound annual growth rate of 3% a year. The largest increase occurred from 2008 to 2009 when participation in food gardening increased by 4 million households, or 11% in one year.[4]

This heightened interest in agricultural self-sufficiency is just one important issue associated with agriculture. Two other increasingly significant issues are whether current agricultural practices can keep up with growing world populations and the ability of the agricultural industry to provide safe, nutritious food to all. Another major concern is whether these systems can be environmentally sustainable while accomplishing these goals.

On a global scale, there have been great strides made in the fight against hunger. Some experts say that the proportion of people suffering from hunger worldwide has fallen by 200 million since 1990, while the world population has increased by 2 billion during the same period.[5] But what will happen as the world population increases?

According to the Chicago Council on Global Affairs:

The world population is expected to reach 8.6 billion in 2030 and 9.8 billion in 2050. Most of the growth is forecast to take place in low-and middle-income countries. If global population reaches 9.1 billion by 2050, based on FAO's report, the world food production will need to rise by 70 percent, and food production in low-and middle-income countries will need to double.[6]

Opinions vary, but there is evidence that some agricultural yields are increasing. In spring of 2019, then Secretary of State Mike Pompeo spoke at a farm meeting in Iowa and congratulated American farmers on the job they were doing by producing astonishing food harvests.[7] It was also noted that the US is the world's top agricultural exporter and will work to continue to be in the future.

On the flip side, concerned individuals are sounding the alarm about the issue of environmental sustainability. "Sustainable agriculture" is a movement away from the industrial method of food production that came about in the twentieth century. Experts warn that industrial agriculture and its pesticides, monocultures, and other defining characteristics are responsible for a variety of problems, including a loss of biodiversity, polluted water and soil resources, deforestation, and more. Proponents of sustainable agriculture support an array of new practices to take their place, including organic, free-range, and regenerative farming.

Americans and people around the world are currently being faced with another major question: are family farms obsolete? Many Americans have nostalgic feelings toward the family farm, imagining a family tending their animals and fields in a bucolic setting. Wisconsin—a Midwestern US state often referred to as "America's Dairyland"—is a microcosm of this controversy. In 2018, the average dairy cow herd contained about 150 animals, with some operations having less and some more. These are considered to be small farms and are often operated by families. Concentrated animal feeding operations—CAFOs—run by industrial farms are overtaking these smaller operations, however.[8] They have cow herds numbering from 700 heads of cattle to over 5,000. Some assert that CAFOs edge family farmers out of the business of farming, which they assert is detrimental to entire communities. Beyond that, the challenge of disposing the massive amounts of animal waste generated by CAFOs demonstrates why industrial farms are criticized for their environmental impact. An alternative way of farming lives on in other parts of the world, however, where small family farms continue to thrive and positively impact their communities.

How can society deal with these agricultural issues and others? Will governmental regulation solve the problems? People in the private sector and in government express the need for more regulation in certain areas, such as control over CAFOs and other industrial farming operations, the overseeing of genetically modified agricultural products (GMOs), and the care of livestock animals. Others disagree and maintain that over-regulation will only prevent the growth of agriculture, which is necessary to provide for future populations. Readers are given the opportunity to contemplate the current debate that surrounds this topic in *Current Controversies: Agriculture* through considering viewpoints that shed light on this ongoing contemporary issue.

Notes

1. "Agriculture," *Merriam-Webster*, https://www.merriam-webster.com/dictionary/agriculture.

2. "Farmer," *Merriam-Webster*, https://www.merriam-webster.com/dictionary/farmer.

3. "Garden to Table: A 5-Year Look at Food Gardening in America," National Gardening Association, 2014, https://garden.org/special/pdf/2014-NGA-Garden-to-Table.pdf.

4. *Ibid.*

5. Linda Poon, "There Are 200 Million Fewer Hungry People Than 25 Years Ago," NPR, June 1, 2015, https://www.npr.org/sections/goatsandsoda/2015/06/01/411265021/there-are-200-million-fewer-hungry-people-than-25-years-ago.

6. Jijung Wang, "Population Growth and World Agriculture Production in the Context of Climate Change," the Chicago Council on Global Affairs, June 26, 2019, https://www.thechicagocouncil.org/blog/global-food-thought/population-growth-and-world-agriculture-production-context-climate-change.

7. David Pitt, "Pompeo Asks Iowa Farmers to Stand Firm With Trump on Trade," *US News and World Report,* March 4, 2019, https://www.usnews.com/news/best-states/iowa/articles/2019-03-04/pompeo-in-iowa-touting-trump-policies-to-farmers.

8. Carrie Hribar, "Understanding Concentrated Animal Feeding Operations and Their Effect on Communities," National Association of Local Boards of Health, 2010, https://www.cdc.gov/nceh/ehs/docs/understanding_cafos_nalboh.pdf.

CHAPTER 1

Does the Global Agricultural System Meet and Secure Nutritional Needs?

Food Security on a Global Scale

United Nations

The United Nations (UN) is an international organization that was founded in 1945 and is currently made up of 193 member states. The UN is dedicated to tackling issues of concern to all humanity.

As the world population continues to grow, much more effort and innovation will be urgently needed in order to sustainably increase agricultural production, improve the global supply chain, decrease food losses and waste, and ensure that all who are suffering from hunger and malnutrition have access to nutritious food. Many in the international community believe that it is possible to eradicate hunger within the next generation, and are working together to achieve this goal.

World leaders at the 2012 Conference on Sustainable Development (Rio+20) reaffirmed the right of everyone to have access to safe and nutritious food, consistent with the right to adequate food and the fundamental right of everyone to be free from hunger. The UN Secretary-General's Zero Hunger Challenge launched at Rio+20 called on governments, civil society, faith communities, the private sector, and research institutions to unite to end hunger and eliminate the worst forms of malnutrition.

The Zero Hunger Challenge has since garnered widespread support from many member States and other entities. It calls for:

- Zero stunted children under the age of two
- 100% access to adequate food all year round
- All food systems are sustainable
- 100% increase in smallholder productivity and income
- Zero loss or waste of food

The Sustainable Development Goal to "End hunger, achieve food security and improved nutrition and promote sustainable

"Food security and nutrition and sustainable agriculture," United Nations. Reprinted by permission.

agriculture" (SDG2) recognizes the inter linkages among supporting sustainable agriculture, empowering small farmers, promoting gender equality, ending rural poverty, ensuring healthy lifestyles, tackling climate change, and other issues addressed within the set of 17 Sustainable Development Goals in the Post-2015 Development Agenda.

Beyond adequate calories intake, proper nutrition has other dimensions that deserve attention, including micronutrient availability and healthy diets. Inadequate micronutrient intake of mothers and infants can have long-term developmental impacts. Unhealthy diets and lifestyles are closely linked to the growing incidence of non-communicable diseases in both developed and developing countries.

Adequate nutrition during the critical 1,000 days from beginning of pregnancy through a child's second birthday merits a particular focus. The Scaling-Up Nutrition (SUN) Movement has made great progress since its creation five years ago in incorporating strategies that link nutrition to agriculture, clean water, sanitation, education, employment, social protection, health care and support for resilience.

Extreme poverty and hunger are predominantly rural, with smallholder farmers and their families making up a very significant proportion of the poor and hungry. Thus, eradicating poverty and hunger are integrally linked to boosting food production, agricultural productivity and rural incomes.

Agriculture systems worldwide must become more productive and less wasteful. Sustainable agricultural practices and food systems, including both production and consumption, must be pursued from a holistic and integrated perspective.

Land, healthy soils, water and plant genetic resources are key inputs into food production, and their growing scarcity in many parts of the world makes it imperative to use and manage them sustainably. Boosting yields on existing agricultural lands, including restoration of degraded lands, through sustainable agricultural practices would also relieve pressure to clear forests for agricultural production. Wise management of scarce water through improved irrigation and storage technologies, combined with development of new drought-resistant crop varieties, can contribute to sustaining drylands productivity.

Halting and reversing land degradation will also be critical to meeting future food needs. The Rio+20 outcome document calls for achieving a land-degradation-neutral world in the context of sustainable development. Given the current extent of land degradation globally, the potential benefits from land restoration for food security and for mitigating climate change are enormous. However, there is also recognition that scientific understanding of the drivers of desertification, land degradation and drought is still evolving.

There are many elements of traditional farmer knowledge that, enriched by the latest scientific knowledge, can support productive food systems through sound and sustainable soil, land, water, nutrient and pest management, and the more extensive use of organic fertilizers.

An increase in integrated decision-making processes at national and regional levels are needed to achieve synergies and adequately address trade-offs among agriculture, water, energy, land and climate change.

Given expected changes in temperatures, precipitation and pests associated with climate change, the global community is called upon to increase investment in research, development and demonstration of technologies to improve the sustainability of food systems everywhere. Building resilience of local food systems will be critical to averting large-scale future shortages and to ensuring food security and good nutrition for all.

American Farmers Feed the World

Dan Charles

Dan Charles is a correspondent for NPR covering the food industry and farming. He was previously a technology correspondent, a freelance writer, and a radio producer.

When critics of industrial agriculture complain that today's food production is too big and too dependent on pesticides, that it damages the environment and delivers mediocre food, there's a line that farmers offer in response: We're feeding the world.

It's high-tech agriculture's claim to the moral high ground. Farmers say they farm the way they do to produce food as efficiently as possible to feed the world.

Charlie Arnot, a former public relations executive for food and farming companies, now CEO of the Center for Food Integrity, says it's more than just a debating point. "U.S. farmers have a tremendous sense of pride in the fact that they've been able to help feed the world," he says.

That phrase showed up, for instance, a few weeks ago at a big farm convention in Decatur, Ill. The seed and chemical company DuPont set up a wall with a question printed at the top in big, capital letters: "How are you making a difference to feed the world?"

The company invited people to answer that question, and thousands of them did. They wrote things like "raising cattle," "growing corn and beans," "plant as much as possible."

Kip Tom, who grows corn and soybeans on thousands of acres of Indiana farmland, says he's very aware of the fact that the world has more and more people, demanding more food. Yet there are fewer and fewer farmers, "and it's the duty of those of us who are left in the business, us family farmers, to help feed that world."

That means growing more food per acre, he says, which requires new and better technology: genetically engineered seed, for instance, or pesticides.

And this is why the words "feed the world" grate on the nerves of people who believe that large-scale, technology-driven agriculture is bad for the environment and often bad for people.

Margaret Mellon, a scientist with the environmental advocacy group Union of Concerned Scientists, recently wrote an essay in which she confessed to developing an allergy to that phrase. "If there's a controversy, the show-stopper is supposed to be, 'We have to use pesticides, or we won't be able to feed the world!' " she says.

Mellon says it's time to set that idea aside. It doesn't answer the concerns that people have about modern agriculture—and it's not even true.

American-style farming doesn't really grow food for hungry people, she says. Forty percent of the biggest crop—corn— goes into fuel for cars. Most of the second-biggest crop—soybeans— is fed to animals.

Growing more grain isn't the solution to hunger anyway, she says. If you're really trying to solve that problem, there's a long list of other steps that are much more important. "We need to empower women; we need to raise incomes; we need infrastructure in the developing world; we need the ability to get food to market without spoiling."

It seemed that this dispute needed a referee. So I called Christopher Barrett, an economist at Cornell University who studies international agriculture and poverty.

"They're both right," he says, chuckling. "Sometimes the opposite of a truth isn't a falsehood, but another truth, right?"

It's true, he says, that bigger harvests in the U.S. tend to make food more affordable around the world, and "lower food prices are a good thing for poor people."

For instance, Chinese pigs are growing fat on cheap soybean meal grown by farmers in the U.S. and Brazil, and that's one reason why hundreds of millions of people in China are eating much better than a generation ago—they can afford to buy pork. So American farmers who grow soybeans are justified in saying that they help feed the world.

But Mellon is right, too, Barrett says. The big crops that American farmers send abroad don't provide the vitamins and minerals that billions of people need most. So if the U.S. exports lots of corn, driving down the cost of cornmeal, "it induces poor families to buy lots of cornmeal, and to buy less in the way of leafy green vegetables, or milk," that have the key nutrients. In this case, you're feeding the world, but not solving the nutrition problems.

Arnot, from the Center for Food Integrity, recently did a survey, asking consumers whether they think the U.S. even has a responsibility to provide food to the rest of the world. Only 13 percent of these consumers strongly agreed.

In focus groups, many people said that if feeding the world means more industrial-scale farming, they're not comfortable with it.

This is not a message farmers like to hear. "It is a real sense of frustration for farmers that 'feeding the world' is no longer a message that resonates with the American public," Arnot says.

He tells farm groups that they'll have to find another message. They'll need to show that the way they grow food is consistent with the values of American consumers.

Changes in Agricultural Practices Will Help to Feed Future Population

Janet Ranganathan, Richard Waite, Tim Searchinger, and Craig Hanson

The authors all work at the World Resources Institute. Janet Ranganathan is vice president of science and research, Richard Waite is an associate, Tim Searchinger is a senior fellow, and Craig Hanson is vice president of food, forest, water, and ocean.

There is a big shortfall between the amount of food we produce today and the amount needed to feed everyone in 2050. There will be nearly 10 billion people on Earth by 2050—about 3 billion more mouths to feed than there were in 2010. As incomes rise, people will increasingly consume more resource-intensive, animal-based foods. At the same time, we urgently need to cut greenhouse gas (GHG) emissions from agricultural production and stop conversion of remaining forests to agricultural land.

Feeding 10 billion people *sustainably* by 2050, then, requires closing three gaps:

- A 56 percent food gap between crop calories produced in 2010 and those needed in 2050 under "business as usual" growth;
- A 593 million-hectare land gap (an area nearly twice the size of India) between global agricultural land area in 2010 and expected agricultural expansion by 2050; and
- An 11-gigaton GHG mitigation gap between expected agricultural emissions in 2050 and the target level needed to hold global warming below 2°C (3.6°F), the level necessary for preventing the worst climate impacts.

"How to Sustainably Feed 10 Billion People by 2050, in 21 Charts," by Janet Ranganathan, Richard Waite, Tim Searchinger, and Craig Hanson, World Resources Institute, December 5, 2018. Reprinted by permission.

A Five-Course Menu of Solutions for a Sustainable Food Future

There is no silver bullet to close the food, land and GHG mitigation gaps. WRI research on how to create a sustainable food future has identified 22 solutions that need to be simultaneously applied to close these gaps. The relative importance of each solution varies from country to country. The solutions are organized into a five-course menu: (1) reduce growth in demand for food and other agricultural products; (2) increase food production without expanding agricultural land; (3) protect and restore natural ecosystems; (4) increase fish supply; and (5) reduce GHG emissions from agricultural production.

First Course: Reduce Growth In Demand for Food and Other Agricultural Products

Reduce Food Loss and Waste

Approximately one-quarter of food produced for human consumption goes uneaten. Loss and waste occurs all along the food chain, from field to fork. Reducing food loss and waste by 25 percent by 2050 would close the food gap by 12 percent, the land gap by 27 percent and the GHG mitigation gap by 15 percent. Actions to take include measuring food waste, setting reduction targets, improving food storage in developing countries and streamlining expiration labels.

Shift to Healthier, More Sustainable Diets

Consumption of ruminant meat (beef, lamb and goat) is projected to rise 88 percent between 2010 and 2050. Beef, the most commonly consumed ruminant meat, is resource-intensive to produce, requiring 20 times more land and emitting 20 times more GHGs per gram of edible protein than common plant proteins, such as beans, peas and lentils. Limiting ruminant meat consumption to 52 calories per person per day by 2050—about 1.5 hamburgers per week—would reduce the GHG mitigation gap by half and nearly close the land gap. In North America this would require reducing current beef and lamb consumption by nearly half. Actions to take include improving the marketing of plant-based foods, improving meat substitutes and implementing policies that favor consumption of plant-based foods.

Avoid Competition from Bioenergy for Food Crops and Land

If bioenergy competes with food production by using food or energy crops or dedicated land, it widens the food, land and GHG mitigation gaps. Biomass is also an inefficient energy source: Using all the harvested biomass on Earth in the year 2000—including crops, crop residues, grass eaten by livestock and wood—would only provide about 20 percent of global energy needs in 2050. Phasing out existing biofuel production on agricultural lands would reduce the food gap from 56 to 49 percent. Actions to take include eliminating biofuel subsidies and not treating bioenergy as "carbon-neutral" in renewable energy policies and GHG trading programs.

Achieve Replacement-Level Fertility Rates

The food gap is mostly driven by population growth, of which half is expected to occur in Africa, and one third in Asia. Most of the world is close to achieving replacement-level fertility by 2050 (2.1 children per woman). Sub-Saharan Africa is the exception, with a current fertility rate above 5 children per woman and a projected rate of 3.2 in 2050. If sub-Saharan Africa achieved replacement-level fertility rates along with all other regions by 2050, it would close the land gap by one quarter and the GHG mitigation gap by 17 percent while reducing hunger. Actions to take include achieving the three forms of social progress that have led all others to voluntarily reduce fertility rates: increasing educational opportunities for girls, expanding access to reproductive health services, and reducing infant and child mortality so that parents do not need to have as many children to ensure survival of their desired number.

Course Two: Increase Food Production Without Expanding Agricultural Land

Increase Livestock and Pasture Productivity

Livestock production per hectare varies significantly from country to country and is lowest in the tropics. Given that demand for animal-based foods is projected to grow by 70 percent by 2050 and that pastureland accounts for two thirds of agricultural land use, boosting pasture productivity is an important solution. A 25 percent faster increase in the output of meat and milk per hectare of pasture between 2010 and 2050 could close the land gap by 20 percent and the GHG mitigation gap by 11 percent. Actions farmers can take include improving fertilization of pasture, feed quality and veterinary care; raising improved animal breeds; and employing rotational grazing. Governments can set productivity targets and support farmers with financial and technical assistance.

Improve Crop Breeding

Future yield growth is essential to keep up with demand. Conventional breeding, the selection of best-performing crops based on genetic traits, accounted for around half of historical crop yield gains. New advances in molecular biology offer great promise for additional yield gains by making it cheaper and faster to map genetic codes of plants, test for desired DNA traits, purify crop strains, and turn genes on and off. Actions to take include significantly increasing public and private crop-breeding budgets, especially for "orphan crops" like millet and yam, which are regionally important, but not traded globally.

Improve Soil and Water Management

Degraded soils, especially in Africa's drylands, may affect one quarter of the world's cropland. Farmers can boost crop yields in degraded soils—particularly drylands and areas with low carbon— by improving soil and water management practices. For example, agroforestry, or incorporating trees on farms and pastures, can help regenerate degraded land and boost yields. Trial sites in Zambia integrating *Faidherbia albida* trees yielded 88–190 percent more maize than sites without trees. A 20 percent faster increase in crop yields between 2010 and 2050—as a result of improvements in crop breeding and soil and water management—could close the land gap by 16 percent and the GHG mitigation gap by 7 percent. Actions to take include increasing aid agencies' support for rainwater harvesting, agroforestry and farmer-to-farmer education; and reforming tree-ownership laws that impede farmers' adoption of agroforestry. Agencies can also experiment with programs that help farmers rebuild soil health.

Plant Existing Cropland More Frequently
Planting and harvesting existing croplands more frequently, either by reducing fallow land or by increasing "double cropping" (planting two crops in a field in the same year), can boost food production without requiring new land. Increasing annual cropping intensity by 5 percent beyond the 2050 baseline of 87 percent would shrink the land gap by 14 percent and the GHG mitigation gap by 6 percent. Researchers should conduct more spatially explicit analyses to determine where cropping intensity increases are most feasible, factoring in water, emissions and other environmental constraints.

Adapt to Climate Change
The 2014 Intergovernmental Panel on Climate Change report projected that without adaptation, global crop yields will likely decline by at least 5 percent by 2050, with steeper declines by 2100. For example, growing seasons in much of sub-Saharan Africa are projected to be more than 20 percent shorter by 2100. A 10 percent decline in crop yields would increase the land gap by 45 percent. Adaptation will require implementing other menu items, as well as breeding crops to cope with higher temperatures, establishing water conservation systems, and changing production systems where major climate changes will make it impossible to grow certain crops.

Course Three: Protect and Restore Natural Ecosystems and Limit Agricultural Land-Shifting

Link Productivity Gains with Protection of Natural Ecosystems

While improving agricultural productivity can save forests and savannas globally, in some cases it can actually cause more land clearing locally. To avoid these results, productivity gains must be explicitly linked with efforts to protect natural ecosystems from conversion to agriculture. Governments, financiers and others can tie low interest credit to protection of forests, as Brazil has done, and ensure that infrastructure investments do not come at the expense of ecosystems.

Limit Inevitable Cropland Expansion to Lands with Low Environmental Opportunity Costs

When cropland expansion is inevitable—such as for local food production in Africa and for oil palm in Southeast Asia—governments and investors should support expansion onto land with low environmental opportunity costs. This includes lands with limited biodiversity or carbon storage potential, but high food production potential. For example, analysis that applies environmental, economic and legal filters in Indonesia can develop more accurate estimates of land suitable for oil palm expansion. Governments need tools and models to estimate yields and effects on biodiversity and climate change, and they should use these tools to guide land-use regulations, plan roads and manage public lands.

Reforest Agricultural Lands with Little Intensification Potential

In some cases, the most efficient use of land may be to restore abandoned or unproductive agricultural lands back into forests or other natural habitats. This can help offset the inevitable expansion of agriculture into other areas. This should be limited to low productivity agricultural land with limited improvement potential, such as steeply sloping pastures in Brazil's Atlantic Forest.

Conserve and Restore Peatlands

Peatlands' conversion for agriculture requires drainage, which releases large amounts of carbon into the atmosphere. The world's 26 million hectares of drained peatlands account for 2 percent of annual greenhouse gas emissions. Restoring them to wetlands should be a high priority and would close the GHG mitigation gap by up to 7 percent. Actions to take include providing funds for peatland restoration, improving peatland mapping and establishing laws that prevent peatlands from being drained.

Course Four: Increase Fish Supply

Improve Wild Fisheries Management

One third of marine stocks were overfished in 2015, with another 60 percent fished at maximum sustainable levels. Catches need to be reduced today to allow wild fisheries to recover enough just to maintain the 2010 fish-catch level in 2050. This would avoid the need to convert 5 million hectares of land to supply the equivalent amount of fish from aquaculture. Actions to take include implementing catch shares and community-based management systems, and removing perverse subsidies that support overfishing, estimated at $35 billion annually.

Improve Productivity and Environmental Performance of Aquaculture

As wild fish catches decline, aquaculture production needs to more than double to meet a projected 58 percent increase in fish consumption between 2010 and 2050. This doubling requires improving aquaculture productivity and addressing fish farms' current environmental challenges, including conversion of wetlands, use of wild-caught fish in feeds, high freshwater demand and water pollution. Actions to take include selective breeding to improve growth rates of fish, improving feeds and disease control, adoption of water recirculation and other pollution controls, better spatial planning to guide new farms and expansion of marine-based fish farms.

Course Five: Reduce Greenhouse Gas Emissions from Agriculture Production

GHG emissions from agricultural production arise from livestock farming, application of nitrogen fertilizers, rice cultivation and energy use. They're projected to rise from 7 to 9 gigatons per year or more by 2050 (in addition to 6 gigatons per year or more from land-use change). This course addresses each of these major emissions sources.

Reduce Enteric Fermentation Through New Technologies

Ruminant livestock were responsible for around half of all agricultural production emissions in 2010. Of these emissions, the largest source is "enteric methane," or cow burps. Increasing productivity of ruminants also reduces methane emissions, mainly because more milk and meat is produced per kilogram of feed. In addition, new technologies can reduce enteric fermentation. For example, 3-nitrooxypropan (3-NOP), a chemical additive that inhibits microbial methane, was tested in New Zealand and cut methane emissions by 30 percent and may increase animal growth rates. Governments should expand public research into compounds like 3-NOP and require or incentivize adoption of the most promising.

Reduce Emissions Through Improved Manure Management

Emissions from "managed" manure, originating from animals raised in confined settings, represented around 9 percent of agricultural production emissions in 2010. Improving manure management by better separating liquids from solids, capturing methane, and other strategies can greatly reduce emissions. For example, using highly sophisticated systems to reduce virtually all forms of pollution from U.S. pig farms would only increase the price of pork by 2 percent while reducing GHGs and creating many health, water and pollution benefits. Measures governments can take include regulating farms, providing competitive funding for technology development, and establishing monitoring programs to detect and remediate leakages from digesters.

Reduce Emissions from Manure Left on Pasture

Livestock feces and urine deposited in fields turns into nitrous oxide, a potent greenhouse gas. This unmanaged manure accounted for 12 percent of agricultural production emissions in 2010. Emerging approaches involve applying chemicals that prevent nitrogen from turning into nitrous oxide, and growing grasses that prevent this process naturally. Governments can increase support for research into such chemical and biological nitrification inhibitors and incentivize adoption by farmers.

Reduce Emissions from Fertilizers by Increasing Nitrogen Use Efficiency

Emissions from fertilizers accounted for around 19 percent of agricultural production emissions in 2010. Globally, crops absorb less than half the nitrogen applied as fertilizer, with the rest emitted to the atmosphere or lost as run off. Increasing nitrogen use efficiency, the percentage of applied nitrogen absorbed by crops, involves improving fertilizers and their management—or the composition of the fertilizers themselves—to increase the rate of nitrogen uptake, thus reducing the amount of fertilizer needed. Actions governments can take include shifting subsidies from fertilizers to support higher nitrogen use efficiency, implementing regulatory targets for fertilizer companies to develop improved fertilizers, and funding demonstration projects that increase nitrogen use efficiency.

Adopt Emissions-Reducing Rice Management and Varieties

Rice paddies contributed at least 10 percent of agricultural production emissions in 2010, primarily in the form of methane. But there are less emissions- and resource-intensive rice production methods. For example, shortening the duration of field flooding can reduce water levels to decrease the growth of methane-producing bacteria. This practice can reduce emissions by up to 90 percent while saving water and increasing rice yields on some farms. Some rice varieties also generate less methane. Actions to take include conducting engineering analyses to identify promising opportunities for reducing water levels, rewarding farmers who practice water-efficient farming, investing in breeding programs that shift to lower-methane rice varieties and boosting rice yields.

Increase Agricultural Energy Efficiency and Shift to Non-Fossil Energy Sources

Emissions from fossil energy use in agriculture accounted for 24 percent of agricultural production emissions in 2010. The basic opportunities include increasing energy efficiency, which has been only modestly explored in agricultural settings, and switching to solar and wind. Reducing emissions per unit of energy used by 75 percent would reduce the GHG mitigation gap by 8 percent. Actions to take include integrating low-carbon energy sources and efficiency programs into agriculture programs and using renewable energy in nitrogen fertilizer manufacturing.

Implement Realistic Options to Sequester Carbon in Soils

Efforts to mitigate agricultural emissions have primarily focused on sequestering carbon in soils, but recent research suggests this is harder to achieve than previously thought. For example, practices to increase carbon, such as no-till farming, produced little or no carbon increases when measured at deeper soil depths. Important strategies include avoiding further loss of carbon from soils by halting conversion of forests, protecting or increasing soil carbon by boosting productivity of grasslands and croplands, increasing agroforestry, and developing innovative strategies for building carbon where soil fertility is critical for food security.

Moving Toward a Sustainable Food Future

The challenge of feeding 10 billion people sustainably by 2050 is much harder than people realize. These menu items are not optional—the world must implement all 22 of them to close the food, land and GHG mitigation gaps.

The good news is that all five courses can close the gaps, while delivering co-benefits for farmers, society and human health. It will require a herculean effort and major changes to how we produce and consume food. So, let's get started and order everything on the menu!

Exciting Developments Increase Agricultural Production

Charles Orton-Jones

Charles Orton-Jones is a freelance writer, editor, and former PPA Business Writer of the Year.

Food production needs to increase by 70 per cent to feed the nine billion population projected for 2050. Fortunately, the industry is benefiting from some radical thinking. Here are the cutting edge technologies taking farming towards this goal.

Bees As Micro-Distributors of Pesticide

Bee Vectoring Technologies is a Canadian startup which has developed a commercial alternative to spraying food crops with pesticide. This innovative new method uses bumblebees to distribute a naturally occurring, organic, inoculating fungus while carrying out their natural foraging cycle.

The BVT system makes commercially reared bumblebees through a specialist tray dispenser as they leave their hive. They brush past a powder which clings to their fur. The powder is a naturally occurring fungus named clonostachys rosea which, when absorbed by a plant, enables it to effectively block destructive diseases, such as botrytis, in strawberries.

The process has many merits. It reduces or negates the need for spraying pesticides, thus preventing chemicals entering the water supply.

In a large-scale trial in Florida it delivered comparable or improved disease protection over sprayed chemicals, as well as increasing fruit yield by between 7 and 29 per cent. This fruit was independently shown to be sweeter and had a longer shelf life.

"The Future of Farming: Robots, Bees, and Plant Jacuzzis," by Charles Orton-Jones, Agritecture Consulting, November 15, 2018. Reprinted by permission.

In a recent trial on blueberries in Nova Scotia, yield increases were recorded at 77 per cent. And the bees, of course, are entirely unharmed.

Vertical Farming

Vertical farming has been around for a while, but recently has begun to scale dramatically.

A new scheme based in North Lincolnshire by Jones Food Company and Current, a division of General Electric, will be the largest indoor farm in Europe, producing up to 420 tonnes of leafy greens per year across a growing area of 5,120 m^2 (equivalent to 26 tennis courts) arranged in racks rising to the height of 11m.

GE's role is to install more than 12km of its Arize LED horticultural bar lights, which offer a balanced light spectrum that catalyses growth and shortens the growth cycle. The facility is housed in a clean environment, so crops are grown in isolation from contamination. This makes it ideal for the beauty and pharmaceutical industries.

It will use up to 90 per cent less water and 50 per cent less fertiliser than conventional growing methods, saving on input costs.

Food production needs to increase by 70 per cent to feed the nine billion population projected for 2050.

Radical Efficiency Boosters

Phytoponics is a Cardiff-based company looking to revolutionise the efficiency of commercial greenhouses. Phytoponics grows vine crops, such as peppers and tomatoes, in an inflatable bag filled with water, which is attached to a pump to filter in nutrients and aerate the water.

The grow bag is made of a flexible polymer which offers high performance, but is cheaper to transport and install than regular hydroponics systems. Founder Adam Dixon calls it a "jacuzzi in a bag," and claims it uses 80 per cent less water than soil-based farming.

Phytoform Labs uses gene-editing technologies to reduce carbon emissions in the agriculture industry. It does this by engineering specific plant traits and characteristics and then breeding them into the plants, so that their cultivation becomes more efficient and less energy intensive.

For example, plants that have traditionally only been grown outdoors—and therefore emitted more carbon—may have their genes modified to allow them to be farmed more efficiently inside greenhouses.

Both of these innovative companies are startups, and received funding from the Shell Livewire programme, normally focused on mainstream tech.

Arrival of the Robot Army

We all know the robots are coming to automate farming. But the extent of the progress being made may surprise farmers.

Projects such as the "Hands Free Hectare" have shown that barley can be grown entirely without human interference. A PhD student at King's College London has developed the Growbot, which lets farm workers with no technology skills program it to perform manual tasks. The project has ongoing funding from the Agriculture & Horticulture Development Board.

In the dairy industry, Universal Robots makes a robot arm able to automate labour-intensive tasks such as manually disinfecting cows' udders before and after being milked.

Perhaps the trickiest area is fruit picking. Rosberg Green House is utilising a universal robot gripper to pick herbs and flowers. The two "fingers" of the robot gripper have built-in intelligence and advanced technology that mimics the way humans instinctively use our sense of touch when we grab things to move them. This means that the delicate produce is not harmed during this process.

Also worth mentioning are robots made by Autostix and ISO Group, which are able to take cuttings. At the current rate of progress, automated farms could be mainstream within the next five years.

Blockchain

Of course, blockchain also gets a mention. The most hyped technology of our era is seen as a potential game-changer in creating trusted and transparent supply chains, and farming could be its ideal market.

Thai Union, the world's largest seafood producer, is partnering with blockchain specialist Eachmile to monitor production from the fishing vessel to shop floor.

There's a clever twist to the project: Etherium-based cryptocurrency Fishcoin is used to incentivise accurate reporting. Workers can be rewarded for correct practices with Fishcoin, and made accountable for issues.

It's early days for blockchain in the supply chain, but with the Chinese government alone investing more than $3 billion since 2016, there's no doubting its potential to the future of farming across the globe.

Food Production Today Is Inherently Unhealthy

Sustainable Life Media, Inc.

Sustainable Brands is a global community that aims to tackle social and environmental challenges.

Hidden killers in food production are making healthy eating impossible for people around the world, according to the Ellen MacArthur Foundation.

According to *Cities and Circular Economy for Food*, excessive use of pesticides, antibiotics in livestock farming, and poor management of fertilizers could lead to 5 million deaths a year globally by 2050—that is twice the current number of deaths caused by obesity and four times the number due to road traffic crashes.

The report, launched today at the World Economic Forum annual meeting in Davos, highlights the enormous environmental damage caused by food production. Synthetic fertilizers, pesticides and mismanaged manure exacerbate air pollution and contaminate soils and water. Food production is currently responsible for almost a quarter of global greenhouse gas emissions.

Even when trying to make healthy food choices, consumers are at risk because of the way food has been produced. To ensure people around the globe can eat healthily, we must not only consider what we eat, but how it is produced. Here, the EMF sets out a vision for a new system—in which food is grown locally and in a way that regenerates natural resources, waste is eliminated through better redistribution and byproduct use, and healthy food is produced without the need for harmful practices.

"The way we produce food today is not only extremely wasteful and damaging to the environment, it is causing serious health

"EMF: Unhealthy Food Production Making Healthy Eating Impossible," Sustainable Life Media, Inc., January 23, 2019. Reprinted by permission.

problems," said Dame Ellen MacArthur. "It cannot continue in the long term; we urgently need to redesign the system."

The report finds that eliminating waste and improving health through a circular economy could be worth US$2.7 trillion a year to the global economy. Health costs caused by pesticide use would decrease by $550 billion a year; and antimicrobial resistance, air pollution, water contamination and food-borne diseases would reduce significantly. Greenhouse gas emissions would be expected to decrease by 4.3 Gt CO2e, the equivalent of taking one billion cars off the road permanently. The degradation of 15 million hectares of arable land would be prevented and 450 trillion liters of fresh water saved annually.

Cities are key to this food revolution: By 2050, they will consume 80 percent of food, giving them the power to drive the shift to this healthy system. Cities themselves can unlock US$700 billion a year by using organic materials to help produce new food and products, and by reducing edible food waste.

The publication of *Cities and Circular Economy for Food* follows the launch yesterday of another EMF report that examines how artificial intelligence could be applied to create a regenerative, circular economy for food and agriculture; as well as last week's release of the EAT-Lancet Commission on Food, Planet, Health.

Dr. Gunhild Stordalen, founder and executive chair of EAT, said: "We cannot achieve a healthy planet and healthy population without a fundamental transformation of our entire food system. *Cities and Circular Economy for Food* describes an approach starting with cities and presents a vision of a future where the way we produce and consume food contributes to environmental and health benefits, instead of damaging human health and the environment. Achieving this is urgent, but no quick fix will get us there. We do have the knowledge and tools to act—and the circular economy approach will be a critical component."

The report was written with analytical support from SYSTEMIQ. Founder and managing partner Martin Stuchtey said: "As pressures on the food system continue to mount—expanding urbanisation, doubling of food demand, increasing food waste, and growing health, environmental and economic costs—it is time to step back and reconsider our actions. The concept of a circular and regenerative food system offers entirely new solutions, driven by reconnecting urban consumers with food production. Our analysis shows this is an economically attractive opportunity we cannot afford to ignore."

The report was made possible by philanthropic partners Calouste Gulbenkian Foundation, players of People's Postcode Lottery and Porticus; in collaboration with lead partners Intesa Sanpaolo and Intesa Sanpaolo Innovation Center; and core partners Danone, Sitra, Suez, Tetra Pak and Veolia.

Cities and Circular Economy for Food is an affiliate project of the World Economic Forum's Platform for Accelerating the Circular Economy (PACE). The report has been produced as part of Project Mainstream, a CEO-led global initiative created by the Ellen MacArthur Foundation and the World Economic Forum, which helps to scale business-driven circular economy innovations.

Key Data and Examples

For every US$1 spent on food, society pays $2 in health, environmental and economic costs. These negative impacts cost $5.7 trillion each year—as much as obesity, malnutrition, and other food consumption issues combined. These costs are related to:

- **Extraction of finite resources:** Vast amounts of phosphorus, potassium, and other finite resources are used in farming. From tractors on the field to food-processing plants and fleets of distribution trucks, most activities in the food system still rely on fossil fuels. For every calorie of food consumed in the US, the equivalent energy of 13 calories of oil are burned to produce it.
- **Waste:** Today, aside from our thousands of tons of preventable food waste each year, less than 2 percent of the valuable nutrients in food by-products and human waste in cities are valorized safely and productively. Instead, these

nutrients are typically destined for landfill, incinerators or, worse, languish in open dumps or are released untreated, where they pose health hazards to nearby residents and the environment.

- **Pollution:** Pesticides and synthetic fertilizers used in conventional farming practices, along with mismanagement of manure, can exacerbate air pollution, contaminate soils, and leach chemicals into water supplies. Poor management of food waste and by-products generated during food processing, distribution, and packaging further pollutes water, particularly in emerging economies. The agrifood industry is the world's second-largest emitter of greenhouse gases, responsible for about 25 percent of all human-caused emissions.

- **Degradation of natural capital:** Each year, poor agricultural practices degrade natural capital—15 million hectares of arable land are lost; approximately 70 percent of global freshwater demand is used for agriculture; and the industry was responsible for about 73 percent of deforestation between 2000 and 2010.

If Nothing Changes?

Air pollution and water contamination, along with antimicrobial resistance exacerbated by antibiotics use in animal farming and inadequately treated wastewaters, could contribute to the aforementioned 5 million deaths a year globally by 2050. The food system alone will have used up two-thirds of the remaining global carbon budget remaining to have a reasonable chance of limiting global warming to 1.5°C or less compared to pre-industrial levels.

Many People in the World Go Hungry

Hilal Elver

Since 2014, Hilal Elver has been the special rapporteur of food issues for the United Nations Human Rights Council.

The greatest challenge for the sustainable development goals (SDGs) is to eradicate poverty and hunger while maintaining sustainable food security for all in a crowded and dramatically unequal world. Although the world has succeeded in reducing poverty in accordance with the millennium development goal (MDG) targets, food security and adequate nutrition have not been achieved.

The MDGs failed to treat food as a human right. Experience shows us that neither markets nor governments protect access to sufficient and nutritious food for everyone. Only accountability by those who produce food and regulate society can hope to achieve this protection, and this means that access to food needs to be treated as a human right, and not just as a policy goal or an outcome of a productive economy. Several constitutions and courts in Latin America have recently moved in this direction by making the right to food a legally enforceable right, but the international system, including the UN, still lags behind.

According to the Food and Agriculture Organisation (FAO), almost 1 billion people suffer from chronic hunger and almost 2 billion are under- or overnourished.

Children are the most visible victims of nutritional deficiencies. Approximately 5 million children die each year because of poor nutrition. Access to adequate food during the first 1,000 days of life is vitally important for healthy future generations. Even a temporary lack of food during that crucial time has a negative effect on physical and intellectual development. I was shocked when told that in Haiti, even before the devastating earthquake that ruined the country, that small mud balls were being sold in the market to ease children's hunger pangs.

Of the world's hungry people, 98% live in developing countries. The root causes of food insecurity and malnutrition are poverty and inequity rather than shortages. FAO statistics confirm that the world produces enough food to feed the 7 billion people living today, and even the estimated 9-10 billion population in 2050. Global agriculture produces 17% more calories per person today than 30 years ago, despite a 70% increase in population.

Despite this, for the 2 billion people making less than $2 a day—many of whom live in rural areas where resource-poor farmers cultivate small plots of land—most can't afford to buy food. It is the economic system that is responsible for this prevalence of poverty and hunger. Recently, climate change has been added to the list of causes.

Smallholder farmers tell us that this is a lifestyle for them, not a business. When they have had to leave their land for financial reasons, they have never emotionally recovered. I have heard these stories in many places; not only in poor developing countries. It is a global phenomenon.

If the international community is serious about eliminating hunger, a shift is needed from a development model based on charity and aid to one based on human rights, reinforced by accountability mechanisms. Marginalised, disempowered and excluded groups previously locked out of development planning must have a place, including minorities, migrants, and poor, disabled, older and indigenous people. Non-discrimination and equality must underpin the entire SDG framework.

The role of women in development and food security is pivotal. Highlighting women's rights in all other targets of the SDGs should be a priority. Of those suffering chronic hunger, 60% are women. This is especially ironic as women do most of the agricultural work in developing countries. Much of the work women do is unpaid and invisible, despite its indispensable role in feeding children and elderly people. Upholding women's financial, educational and legal rights would be the best use of funds dedicated to eradicating hunger, poverty and child undernourishment.

Food security is dependent on the sustainability of food supply. A major effort is needed to avoid practices that exacerbate the negative impacts of food production and consumption on climate, water and ecosystems. The SDGs should make a healthy environment an internationally guaranteed human right.

The SDGs should encourage governments to work towards policy coherence: agricultural policies should be compatible with environmental sustainability and trade rules consistent with food security. This will not be easy to implement. It will require allowing national food markets in developing countries to compete successfully against cheap imported food. It means altering international trade rules to prevent interference with domestic policies in developing countries designed to eradicate hunger and poverty.

Placing human rights at the heart of the SDGs presupposes both a strong accountability framework and the will to enforce this. Transnational corporations can be part of the problem, tending to undermine the livelihood of locals, displacing them from their home and land, interfering with their access to natural resources, and causing environmental destruction. Responsibility for human rights violations must extend to the private sector. International law has traditionally been reluctant to do this. It is encouraging to note that some modest steps have been taken recently to encourage corporate responsibility, including the UN Guiding Principles on Business and Human Rights and Maastricht Principles for Extraterritorial Obligations(pdf). The SDGs could incorporate these documents in their policy guidelines, or adopt their own version.

The new goals should not be allowed to operate as easily ignored principles, but need to be given teeth. We can eradicate poverty, maintain food security and ensure the right to adequate and nutritious food for all. These fundamental aims were long ago set forth in the Universal Declaration of Human Rights, and repeated in the International Covenant of the Economic, Social and Cultural Rights. The task is huge, but the tools are there. The challenge is mainly a matter of fashioning political will strong enough to overcome entrenched interests in maintaining food insecurity.

In Southern Asia, Malnutrition and Hunger Are Common

ReliefWeb

ReliefWeb is an online source providing reliable and timely information focused on global crises and disasters.

The Asian Legal Resource Centre (ALRC) wishes to highlight failures by the Bangladeshi, Indian and Nepalese governments in ensuring their citizen's right to food. All three are State Parties to the International Covenant on Economic, Social, and Cultural Rights (ICESCR), which guarantees the right to food as a fundamental right under article 11, but also have amongst the highest rates of child malnutrition and maternal mortality in Asia. These governments are depriving vulnerable groups from accessing resources, land and food; in particular landless Dalits (low caste communities in South Asia) and indigenous groups.

India

The Prime Minister announced in 2010 that the child malnutrition and starvation was not acceptable. However, the government has not given priority to food security and in fact contributes to many of the causes of widespread hunger. The National Food Security Act drafted in January 2011 fails to cover all of the poor in rural areas and introduces a weak mechanism for punishment of corrupt officials, which has been the root cause of the failure of the enforcement of various previous policies and programs related to the right to food for the poor. Rotten food grains found in several states in 2010, that should have been delivered to the poor, shows that poor governance is another important aspect that contributes to the government's failure to fulfill the right to food.

"South Asia: Poor governance and corruption in Bangladesh, India and Nepal leading to child malnutrition and widespread hunger," ReliefWeb, February 17, 2011. Reprinted by permission.

Child malnutrition cases documented in Madhya Pradesh expose the lack of government systems to ensure redress and lack of political will to ensure food self-sufficiency for the poor. In districts such as Sahariya, Rewa, Satna, Jhabua and Khandwa, more than 60% of the children are undernourished, and around 20 percent face severe acute malnutrition. High levels of child malnutrition have persisted for years here. Communities facing child malnutrition belong to tribes or Dalits confronting discrimination and corruption. The government's responses has been pitiful, and do not address the main causes of child malnutrition, instead often resorting to denial about the fact that malnutrition is behind the deaths of children. Emergency distribution measures typically fail to reach many malnourished children and the State is failing to put in place community-based health care systems that could prevent the recurrence of such emergencies.

Farmers are being forced to cultivate ever-smaller areas of land or even evicted from their land completely, engendering poverty and hunger. The government and third parties are taking over natural resources, including land, in the name of development' leading to scarcity of food. Poor villagers are being excluded from decision-making process and do not get any benefits from development projects, in violation of domestic laws.

Chutka village, located in Mandla district, Madhya Pradesh, is one of 38 villages predominantly occupied by tribes, where the government and the Nuclear Power Corporation of India Limited have been planning to establish a power plant since 1984. The villagers had previously been displaced during the building of the Bargi dam and now face displacement once again. The villagers were supposed to be provided with electricity following the building of the dam but this has not happened. Some could afford to buy agricultural land in other areas with the compensation provided, however they got much less land than before due to rising land prices.

The recent decision by the Indian Ministry of the Environment and Forests allowing Korean subsidiary Pohang Steel Company

(POSCO)'s steel plant, mining and port project, launched in Orissa, also presents a number of problems including concerning the right to food. In the land acquisition process, over 40,000 villagers were completely excluded from their land and many were also assaulted by the police during a peaceful protest in May 2010. The decision to allow the project to go ahead went against the advice of four out of five committees formed by the Ministry of Environment and Forests. These committees suggested the withdrawal of the project due to its serious impact upon environment and violations of law tribal lands and livelihood. The Ministry chose to go with the recommendation of the one committee that gave the plan a positive response. In addition, the Ministry accepted the statement by the Ministry of Tribal Affairs concerning a land claim by the tribes in the affected areas, which stated that there was no land claim from six villages. This has led to criticism of both ministries.

Nepal

Nepal currently stands at a crossroads in its history and has the opportunity to create new policies and laws, and implement an effective system to guarantee the right to food for all, in particular the most vulnerable groups, such as Dalits and indigenous groups. Key policies concerning land redistribution, construction of infrastructure and food distribution have not been effective to date. Cases documented suggest that the main causes for this are discrimination against Dalits and indigenous groups, and non-transparency and corruption in enforcing policies and laws.

The Lands Act and other laws related to land and agrarian reform have been launched since the early 1960s, but the government has failed to implement them in practice. The government has instead succeeded in nationalizing forestlands that were home to indigenous people, depriving them of the resources that they have been depending on for generations. This has been accompanied by failed land redistribution to the landless. Official data shows that 30 percent of Nepal's rural population are landless, most of whom are Dalits who live in extreme poverty and starvation, whereas 54 percent are tenants on the land. 'Untouchability' has been abolished by law, but remains deeply rooted in a society and the main obstacle in implementing laws and policies aiming at guaranteeing the right to food to vulnerable groups.

The Gandharva community, which numbers 21,000 individuals, is one such Dalit communities facing chronic hunger. 70 percent of the Gandharva are landless. Some have settled along the Manahara river bank in Bardiya district, with only 0.08 acres having been allotted to each household by the government in 1993. The villagers could build houses but struggle to cultivate food on this land. Women are forced to migrate to the Gulf countries as domestic workers and face many serious violations of their rights there, whereas the men migrate to neighbouring countries, as they cannot get jobs due to caste-based discrimination at home. Their wages are not sufficient to support their families, leading to a lack of nutrition and serious health issues, including paralysis amongst their children. Safe drinking water is not available, affecting food safety and health.

The government budget for 2008-9 enabled the establishment of a High Level Scientific Land Reform Commission in order to abolish feudal land ownership. As with many other human rights issues during the current period of political logjam in the country, the government has yet to adopt the recommendations made by the Commission. The 2010-11 budget targets food insecurity zones in Karnali and Mahakali, located in the far western area of Nepal but nothing has happened as yet. Villagers there go through food scarcity every year from February to June. The land is not productive enough to enable self-sufficiency. Earlier, they could cultivate medical plants and apples to get food by trade. However, the government has since blocked the trade route without providing alternatives for their livelihood, leading to starvation and suicides.

In 2010, villagers in Karnali again suffered from hunger during the traditional festival in October, since the government failed to provide subsidized food in time. The price of rice subsidized by the government and delivered by the National Food Corporative is 1.5-2 times higher than in Kathmandu (at 80 Nepali rupees per kilogram) due to transportation difficulties, for which the poor villagers have to pay. The 2010-11 budget earmarked for infrastructure in Karnali has not materialised. The government has also failed to identify the poorest in the regions and instead distributes rice on a first-come-first-served basis. It is more difficult for the poorest, Dalits and the villagers living in the most remote districts, such as Karnali-Jumla, Humla, Kalikot, Mugu and Jumla, to reach towns where rice is disseminated. Dalits often have to wait for all non-Dalits villagers to have collected rice first, resulting in them often returning home without food.

Bangladesh

Bangladesh announced in its official statement on the budget for 2009-10 that the State was self-sufficient in terms of food production. The government, however, violates the right to food of vulnerable groups such as landless farmers, indigenous groups, minorities and women. Paddy farmers account for 69% of the population are the largest occupational sector in country, but many of them are landless and face child malnutrition and food insecurity. For some five months before and after harvest season each year, villagers do not have work and floods or droughts seriously affect cultivation, in particular in Northern Bangladesh.

Mr. Md. Rafiqul Islam has been living without sufficient resources in Gaibandha district, Northern Bangladesh, which is officially known to be the most vulnerable area in terms of food security. He is paid around 80-120 BDT (1.12-1.68 USD) per day for agricultural work only during the working season. The government has yet to set up a minimum wage. The price of staple rice has increased, and is now at around 35-40 BDT per kilogram in this area. His two sons and daughter face a lack of nutrition and his daughter is even deprived of the right to an education. The mostly landless elderly in the district also face a lack of food and healthcare. Cases documented in the district show that corrupt officials do not allow them to enjoy government food distribution and other policies and programs unless they pay bribes.

The budget for basic healthcare facilities has not been sufficiently allocated. Community clinics suffer from a lack of medicine. Social security programs targeting the elderly do not function effectively. Rafiqul's family does not enjoy any support from the government and has to pay bribes to officials and public representatives. Those who can afford to pay bribes often get the benefits although they are not eligible for them. Corruption is amongst the biggest obstacles that hampers food security for the poor here. The local government has responded that they would remedy this by identifying those in greatest need and ensuring government programs reach them, but this has not been witnessed yet.

The Asian Legal Resources Centre Calls Upon the Human Rights Council To:

1. Demand that the governments of Bangladesh, India and Nepal establish mechanisms to clearly identify the poorest persons in the country, and effectively target food aid in their direction, in order to fulfil their right to food with a transparent system that is open to public scrutiny.

2. Encourage these governments to establish complaints mechanism for the poor who are being denied their right to food, in order for them to receive redress.

3. Suggest that the Special Rapporteurs on the rights to food, health and water work together to propose a comprehensive approach that these governments can adopt to tackle child malnutrition and the wider problem of hunger and related disease and deaths in Bangladesh, India and Nepal, as these three States face similar challenges.

CHAPTER 2

Are Family Farms Obsolete?

Family Farms Produce America's Food

James M. MacDonald and Robert A. Hoppe

James M. MacDonald is the former branch chief of the USDA's Economic Research Service (ERS), and Robert A. Hoppe is an agricultural economist for the ERS.

Family farms play a dominant role in U.S. agriculture. In 2015, these farms accounted for 99 percent of U.S. farms and 89 percent of production. On family farms, the principal operators and their relatives (by blood or marriage) own more than half of the business's assets—in short, a family owns and operates the farm.

In 2015, 90 percent of U.S. farms were small family operations with under $350,000 in annual gross cash farm income (GCFI)—a measure of revenue that includes sales of crops and livestock, Government payments, and other farm-related income. These small farms, however, only accounted for 24 percent of the value of production. By comparison, large-scale family farms with at least $1 million in GCFI made up only 2.9 percent of U.S. farms but contributed 42 percent of total production. Nonfamily farms accounted for only 11 percent of agricultural production.

Production has been shifting to larger farms for many years. Family and nonfamily farms with over $1 million in GCFI accounted for half of the value of U.S. farm production in 2015, up from about a third in 1991. That comparison takes account of inflation in farm product prices over time, and therefore reflects shifts of production to larger farms.

The shift has come at the expense of small farms. Small family and nonfamily farms accounted for 46 percent of production in 1991, but by 2015, that share had fallen under 25 percent.

Cropland has also shifted to larger farms. For example, the midpoint size—the farm size that marks the middle of the

"Large Family Farms Continue To Dominate U.S. Agricultural Production," by James M. MacDonald and Robert A. Hoppe, U.S. Department of Agriculture, March 6, 2017.

distribution of cropland—was 589 acres in 1982. This means that half of U.S. cropland was on farms that operated under 589 acres, and the other half was on farms that operated over 589 acres. As cropland shifts to relatively large farms, the midpoint increases—as it has done steadily over the last 30 years—reaching 1,234 acres by 2012. This shift was not only large and persistent but also ubiquitous, occurring in almost all States and for all crops.

Even as the midpoint farm size increased over time, the average (mean) farm size changed little. Among farms with cropland, the average size was 222 acres in 1982, 257 acres in 1992, and 251 acres in 2012. The relative stability in the mean follows from a decline in the number of midsize farms as cropland consolidated into larger operations. This trend, in turn, was offset to a great extent by an increasing number of very small farms (under 20 acres of cropland) since the early 1990s.

The increase in the number of very small farms may reflect more small fruit and vegetable operations. But much of the increase likely reflects improved data collection efforts in the census and USDA surveys since 1997, as well as the effect of inflation. USDA defines a farm as any place that sells or could normally have sold $1,000 worth of agricultural commodities in a year. Average farm commodity prices rose by 94 percent between 2002 and 2012, so a place with $550 in sales in 2002 would not have been counted as a farm. But the same quantity of production would properly have qualified it as a farm in 2012 by reaching the $1,000 sales threshold after price inflation.

Ongoing innovations in agriculture have enabled a single farmer, or farm family, to manage more acres or more animals. Farmers who take advantage of these innovations to expand their operations can reduce costs and raise profits because they can spread their investments over more acres. In 2015, larger family farms displayed stronger financial performance, on average, than smaller farms. For example, 74 percent of very large family farms (GCFI of $5 million or more) had estimated operating profit margins in excess of 10 percent of sales in 2015—compared to

54 percent of midsize family farms (GCFI of $350,000 to $999,999) and 41 percent of moderate-sales small family farms (GCFI of $150,000 to $349,999).

Following these margins over time shows that these differences persist regardless of the performance of the farm sector. Farm sector financial performance has weakened in recent years: ERS estimates that sector net farm income in 2015 was 13 percent lower than in 2014 and 35 percent below the record value of 2013. The persistent gap in financial performance between large and small farms in 2015 indicates that consolidation is likely to continue.

Most large-scale U.S. farms in 2015 were family operations: over 90 percent (about 59,000 farms). Among the 6,300 large nonfamily farms, about 1,760 were organized as corporations, with almost all of the rest organized as partnerships among unrelated individuals; as cooperatives; or as farms operated by hired managers on behalf of trusts, estates, families, or institutions.

Most of the large nonfamily farms that were organized as corporations had 10 or fewer shareholders. Corporations with more than 10 shareholders operated a few hundred large U.S. farms, or about 0.5 percent of all large U.S. farms. Large corporations play an important role in setting procurement standards and organizing supply chains for farm products, but they directly operate very few U.S. farms.

Organic Farms Cannot Produce Enough Food to Feed the Global Population

Rupesh Paudyal

Rupesh Paudyal is a science blogger for TalkPlant.com *and a former researcher. He focuses on science and policy affecting innovation.*

Agriculture helped to build our civilisation; now it threatens to lead the charge to our downfall. Our agriculture system keeps billions alive around the world. But, it's also one of the biggest generators of emissions contributing to the current ecological and climate crisis. Current farming practices cause soil erosion, slowly sucking the life out of the very soil that we grow on. It also pollutes water and air, taking a severe toll on public health.

Our challenge is to produce enough food to feed an increasing world population, which is projected to reach 9.8 billion by 2050, while also protecting the environment and biodiversity. The agriculture industry needs to make drastic changes to its practice to be sustainable. Many believe that adopting and expanding organic farming could make agriculture more environmentally friendly.

On the contrary, organic practice also generates heated debates. Critics argue that environmental benefits of organic farming are outweighed by lower yields that wouldn't be enough to feed the world, and that organic farms would need more land than conventional farms to produce the same amount of food.

At present, organic farming only covers one percent of the global agricultural area. Strict regulations make it harder for the organic industry to expand rapidly. Regulatory logistics aside, if we're to flip the global cropland to organic, we'd have to make radical changes to what we grow. Before we dive in to change global crop production, we must have a good idea of how these changes affect the world. To do this, scientists use available data to generate models that allow us to predict future outcomes.

Previous organic farming models are limited due to simplistic analysis in a small geographic region. Studies so far haven't considered the complexity of crop rotation that would no doubt change crop production. These limitations in current models could be a barrier to wider adoption of organic farming. Limited knowledge from basic models certainly makes the large-scale organic conversion of croplands a much risky affair.

A new study models a "scenario" where all croplands are organic. Scientists modelled the world under the hundred percent organic scenario to generate a high-resolution map showing variances in crop production and yields by factoring in the global differences in crop rotations. The study, led by Dr Pietro Barbieri, used pre-existing data for the sixty-one most important crops that cover ninety-five percent of global cropland use. Researchers then grouped these crops into seven categories to estimate food production under both the current scenario and the hypothetical organic scenario.

Just three plants (rice, wheat and maize) provide over half of the plant-derived calories worldwide. These three plants utilise a significant portion of the global cropland area—and that's a big problem to agriculture biodiversity and food security. Barbieri and colleagues found that total organic agriculture would drastically change what we grow.

Under the total organic scenario, harvested area for primary cereals (for example, rice, wheat and maize) would reduce by over 150 million hectares—a reduction of nearly one-third in comparison to the current agriculture practice. In contrast, there would be a significant increase in global cropland use for secondary cereals (such as spelt and barley) and pulses (for example, soybean and chickpeas). Therefore, global organic farming would produce less of the crops that currently dominate global agriculture, but a greater variety of food will be available. This change will force drastic changes in dietary habits around the world, especially in regions that strongly rely on primary cereals, namely maize, rice and wheat.

"Our analysis predicts that under the hundred percent organic scenario, global calories from primary cereals would decrease by about forty percent. But other crops, especially pulses and secondary cereals, can partially substitute this dietary gap," says Barbieri, who is Associate Professor in Agronomy at Bordeaux Sciences Agro. Increase in agriculture biodiversity would be welcome news both for farmers and consumers. But there is a catch: there wouldn't be enough food for all of us.

Barbieri adds: "Our results suggest that there would be a decrease in calorie production under the hypothetical hundred percent organic scenario." Total organic farming would only produce enough energy to feed 5.9 billion people; conventional agriculture can feed 7.9 billion. As the current world population is just over 7.5 billion, the model predicts that a full conversation to organic farming would mean that there wouldn't be enough food for over 1.6 billion people.

[NOTE: analysis in this paper is for the current population under current agriculture practices; this paper doesn't include any hypothesis on future projections.]

Despite farmers currently producing more than enough to feed the entire population, some 800 million people still go hungry. Total organic could exacerbate that problem. However, Barbieri warns that there is a caveat to the analysis. "We didn't include any change to the amount of food waste and per-capita dietary requirements in our data modelling. Decreasing food waste and a more balanced per-capita energy demand are necessary to guarantee a sufficient global food supply."

The research article, published in *Nature Sustainability*, predicts that under total organic farming, temporary fodders will gain the biggest uptake of cropland use. Temporary fodders currently occupy twelve percent of the total harvested area; under the global organic scenario, temporary fodders will occupy nearly two-thirds more cropland than now—an increase of over 80 million hectares.

Increase in temporary fodder production would ultimately produce more food supply from animal products. Current animal supply feeds around 800 million, but under total organic agriculture, animal supply would feed 900 million people. Livestock farming generates significantly more emissions than plants. Therefore, there is a danger that a surge in global livestock farming fuelled by more temporary fodders production would increase the greenhouse gases emissions.

"Greenhouse emissions may rise if the temporary fodders are used to raise livestock. However, several factors linked conventional agriculture produce such emissions. Our data model hasn't considered factors such as the emission fertiliser industry or the effects of carbon capture by fodders. These factors may reduce net emissions despite an increase in livestock farming. But we need further studies to answer this question," says Barbieri.

In contrast to the global trend, data modelling predicts that total organic agriculture would produce higher energy outputs in a few "hotspots" around the world. And interestingly, these hotspot regions usually fall inside the low producing countries. Barbieri says: "Our estimation suggests that organic farming could boost production in areas where agriculture systems are not strongly industrialised." In line with Barbieri's conclusions, regions with established industry and infrastructure would indeed produce fewer calories under organic farming. However, Barbieri warns that "this generalisation only concerns total calories produced, without considering adverse environmental impact the industrial systems are causing on the agroecosystems."

Our ability to feed the world is intertwined with the environment and ecosystems. With proper management, organic farming could contribute to global food security agriculture without significantly affecting yields, as well as producing a wider array of foods. But as the research shows, there's only so far organic farming takes us. For our future food security, we need to explore every avenue possible to us.

Collaborative Community Farms Can Be More Successful than Family Farms

Sarah Taber

Sarah Taber is a crop scientist and former farmworker. She hosts the podcast "Farm to Taber" on agricultural innovation.

Family farms are central to our nation's identity. Most Americans, even those who have never been on a farm, have strong feelings about the *idea* of family farms—so much that they're the one thing that all U.S. politicians agree on. Each election, candidates across the ideological spectrum roll out plans to save family farms — or give speeches about them, at least. From *Little House on the Prairie* to modern farmer's markets, family farms are also the core of most Americans' vision of what sustainable, just farming is supposed to look like.

But as someone who's worked in agriculture for 20 years and researched the history of farming, I think we need to understand something: Family farming's difficulties aren't a modern problem born of modern agribusiness. It's *never* worked very well. It's simply precarious, and it always has been. Idealizing family farms burdens real farmers with overwhelming guilt and blame when farms go under. It's crushing.

I wish we talked more openly about this. If we truly understood how rare it is for family farms to happen at all, never mind last multiple generations, I hope we could be less hard on ourselves. Deep down we all know that the razor-thin margins put families in impossible positions all the time, but we still treat it like it's the ideal. We blame these troubles on agribusiness—but we don't look deeper. We should. If we're serious about building food systems that are sustainable and robust in the long term, we need to learn from how farming's been done for most of human history: collaboratively.

Farming has almost always existed on a larger social scale— very extended families up to whole villages. We tend to think of medieval peasants as forebears of today's family farms, but they're not. Medieval villages worked much more like a single unit with little truly private infrastructure—draft animals, plows, and even land were operated at the community level. Family farming as we know it— nuclear families that own their land, pass it on to heirs, raise some or all of their food, and produce some cash crops—is vanishingly rare in human history.

It's easy to see how Anglo-Americans could mistake it for normal. Our cultural heritage is one of the few places where this fluke of a farming practice has made multiple appearances. Family farming was a key part of the political economy in ancient Rome, late medieval England, and colonial America. But we keep forgetting something very important about those golden ages of family farming. They all happened after, and *only* after, horrific depopulation events.

Rome emptied newly conquered lands by selling the original inhabitants into slavery. In England, the Black Death killed so many nobles and serfs that surviving peasants seized their own land and became yeomen—free small farmers who neither answered to a master nor commanded their own servants. Colonial Americans, seeking to recreate English yeoman farming, began a campaign of genocide against indigenous people that has lasted for centuries, and created one of the greatest transfers of land and wealth in history.

Family farming isn't just difficult. It's so brittle that it only makes a viable livelihood for farmers when land is nearly valueless for sheer lack of people. In areas where family farming has persisted for more than a couple generations it's largely thanks to extensive, modern technocratic government interventions like grants, guaranteed loans, subsidized crop insurance, free training, tax breaks, suppression of farmworker wages, and more. Family farms' dependence on the state is well understood within the industry, but it's heresy to talk about it openly lest taxpayers catch on. I think it's time to open up, because I don't think a practice that needs that much life support can truly be considered "sustainable." After seeing what I've seen from 20 years in the industry, continuing to present it as such feels to me like a type of con game—because there is a better way.

America's history is filled with examples of collaborative farming. It's just less publicized than single-family homesteading. African-American farmers have a long and determined history of collaborative farming, a brace against the viciousness of slavery and Jim Crow. Native peoples that farmed usually did so as a whole community rather than on a single-family basis. In the early days of the reservation system, some reservations grew their food on one large farm run by the entire nation or tribe. These were so successful that colonial governments panicked, broke them up, and forced indigenous farmers to farm as individual single-family homesteads. This was done with the express goal of impoverishing them—which says a lot about the realities of family farming, security, and financial independence. It also says a lot about how long those grim realities have been understood. Indigenous groups today run modern, innovative, community-level land operations, including over half the farms in Arizona; or Tanka's work restoring prairies, bison, and traditional foodways in the Dakotas as the settler-built wheat economy dries up.

One collaborative tradition that's been very public about how their community-size farms function is the Hutterites, a religious group of about 460 communities in the U.S. and Canada numbering 75-150 people apiece. Despite the harsh prairies where they live, and farming about half as many acres per capita as neighboring family farmers, Hutterites are thriving and expanding when neighboring family farms are throwing in the towel. Their approach—essentially farming as a large employee-owned company with diverse crops and livestock—has valuable lessons.

Outsiders often chalk up the success of the Hutterites, who forgo most private property, to "free labor" or "not having to pay taxes." Neither of these are accurate. Hutterite farms thrive due to farming as a larger community rather than as individual families. Family farms can achieve economies of scale by specializing in one thing, like expanding a dairy herd or crop acreage. But with only one or two family members running a farm, there simply isn't enough bandwidth to run more than one or two operations, no matter how much labor-saving technology is involved. The community at a Hutterite farm allows them to actually pull off what sustainability advocates talk about, but family farms consistently struggle with: diversifying.

To understand why this structure is useful, take the experience of a colleague whose family runs a wheat farm in the Great Plains. He's trying to make extra cash by grazing cattle on their crop when it's young. This can enhance the soil and future yields if done right, and his family agreed to it, but they couldn't help build the necessary fence, or pay for another laborer to help him. The property remains fenceless, without additional income, and without the soil health boosts from carefully managed grazing. Community-size farms like Hutterite operations have larger, more flexible labor pools that don't get stuck in these catch-22 situations.

Stories like this abound in farm country. America's farmland is filled with opportunities to sustainably grow more food from the same acres and earn extra cash, thwarted by the limited attention solo operations can give. We treat this plight as natural and inevitable. We treat it as something to solve by collective action on a national level—government policies that help family farms. We don't talk about how readily these things can be solved by collective action at the local level.

Collaboration doesn't just make better use of the land—it can also do a lot for farmers' quality of life. Hutterites, thanks to farming on a community scale, get four weeks of vacation per year; new mothers get a few months' maternity leave and a full-time helper of their choosing—something few American women in any vocation can do.

We don't have to commit to the Hutterite lifestyle to benefit from the advantages of collaborative farming. Big, diverse, employee-owned farms work, and they can turn farming into a job that anyone can train for and get—you don't have to be born into it.

Many of today's new farmers who weren't born into farming are young and woefully undercapitalized, stuck in a high-labor/ low-revenues cycle with little chance for improvement. Others begin farming as a second career, with plenty of capital but a time horizon of perhaps 20 years—rather than the 40 it often takes to make planting orchards, significant investments in land, and other improvements worth it. These new farmers are absolutely trying to do the right thing, but solo farming simply doesn't give them the resources or time horizon to "think like a cathedral builder." Good farming is a relay race. We have to build human systems that work like a relay team.

Finally, and perhaps most important, collaborative farming can be a powerful tool for decolonization. Hutterite communities are powerhouses, raising most of the eggs, hogs, or turkeys in some states—and they're also largely self-sufficient. This has allowed them to build their own culture to suit their own values. They have enough scale to build their own crop processing, so they can work directly with retailers and customers on their own terms instead of going through middlemen. They build their own knowledge instead of relying on "free" agribusiness advice as many family farms do. In other words, they're powerful. Imagine what groups like this, with determined inclusivity from top leadership down through rank-and-file, could do to right the balance of power in the United States.

Solo farming does work for a few. I don't want to discount their accomplishments—but I also don't think we can give them their due without acknowledging the uphill battle they're in. I think it's important to be honest about family farming's challenges and proactive about handling them. One of the best ways to do that is to pool efforts. Our culture puts so much emphasis on one "right" way of farming—solo family operations—that we ignore valuable lessons from people who've done it differently for hundreds or thousands of years. It's time for us to open up and look at other ways of doing things.

Black Family Farmers Shaped US Agriculture, but Cooperatives May Be Necessary for Survival

Heather Gray

Heather Gray is a writer and radio producer in Atlanta, Georgia. Her work focuses on black farmer issues and cooperative economic development in the rural South.

The 2015 Food Sovereignty Prize will be shared by the Federation of Southern Cooperatives/Land Assistance Fund (Federation) and the Black Fraternal Organization of Honduras. The prize will be presented in Des Moines on October 14, 2015. Thankfully, this prize honors the important work of family farmers throughout the world.

The Food Sovereignty prize was first awarded in 2009 as an alternative to the World Food Prize (also taking place this week in Des Moines, Iowa) founded by "the father of the Green Revolution," the late Norman Borlaug. While the World Food Prize emphasizes increased production through technology, the Food Sovereignty Prize, awarded by the U.S. Food Sovereignty Alliance, champions solutions coming from those most impacted by the injustices of the global food system. In honoring those who are organizing to reclaim local food systems, the commons and community self-determination, the Food Sovereignty Prize affirms that nothing short of the true democratization of our food system will enable us to end hunger once and for all. (EcoWatch)

The theme this year is "Black Farmer's Lives Matter." This is indeed true!

Black farmers have fed their communities and have always generously done so during and since the end of slavery. Much food has almost always been shared with those in need. But the

"Black Farmers' Lives Matter: The significant contributions of Black Farmers in America," by Heather Gray, Free Range, October 14, 2015. Reprinted by permission.

production has been diverse and with a wealth of traditional knowledge through the generations as is true with family farmers throughout the world.

In the late 1990s, I conducted a research project for the Federation that included interviews of farmers throughout the South. I was amazed at the abundance and variety of produce grown by Black farmers. Even if they grew a huge acreage of monocrops, they also tended to maintain an important tradition of a diverse production of fruits and vegetables somewhere on their farm. When farmers have talked with me about the crops they grow, regardless of their struggles, on a consistent basis I have witnessed a gleam in their eyes. It's as if farming is indeed a spiritual experience regardless of who you are or where you are from.

Yet this on-going productivity has never been easy, largely because of southern and national politics, along with the growing industrial systems in agriculture that continue to threaten the integrity of our important family farmer sector.

In fact, since the end of the Civil War in 1865 and prior to that as well, Black farmers have made significant contributions to agriculture in America.

The Freedman's Bureau was created in 1865 to assist freed slaves and poor whites after the Civil War. The Bureau, however, was never given the directive from Congress to offer 40 acres to the Black community but rather small portions of from 10 to 15 acres. Unlike whites that were given free land in the west, thanks to the 1862 Homestead Act, Blacks needed to "purchase" their land. In fact, with the Homestead Act, American whites received some of the most massive welfare subsidies of any people in the world in the nineteenth century. Nevertheless, by the early 1900's the Black community had managed to purchase some 15 million acres of land. It was an amazing feat. Yet by 1910, the loss of black-owned land began with the advent, for one, of Jim Crow laws in the South. Today the acreage farmed by Black farmers is a little over 4.5 million acres.

The contributions of the Black farming community in the development of U.S. food and culture have also been exceptional and likely more than any other ethnic group in the South. Most of the slaves in America came from West Africa and that culture is reflected, for one, in the food we eat today. For centuries, Black farmers have maintained the growth of these traditional foods.

In fact, many of the African foods we eat in the 21st century came with Africans on ships during the slave trade. African origins of some of our foods include okra, gumbo, watermelon, spinach, coffee, yams, black-eyed peas, sorghum, and African rice. All of these foods resonate in the South today.

Okra is thought to be from Ethiopia or also, and more likely, from West Africa where it was also grown and eaten abundantly. The word gumbo is believed to have come from "quingombo," of the word "quillobo," which is the native name for the okra plant in the Congo and Angola areas of Africa. Watermelon is thought to have originated in the Kalahari Desert of Africa and in the 1800s British missionary David Livingston saw an abundance of watermelon growing wild in central Africa. Spinach is from North Africa. Coffee is from Ethiopia. Yams are a staple food in West Africa. It is thought the first domestication of black-eyed peas took place in West Africa. Sorghum and African rice are thought to have come from the Sahel in Africa some 5,000 years ago. African rice has been grown in West Africa for some 3,000 years.

Rice, in fact, was critical to building wealth in the American colonies. For example, white plantation owners in South Carolina did not have a clue about growing rice. They opted to bring in slaves from West Africa where, as mentioned, rice had been grown for thousands of years. It was African women who taught these planation owners, of course, as women were the farmers, as was true throughout most of the African continent. Nevertheless, white South Carolinians still resonate from the wealth they accumulated thanks to the skills and vast knowledge of African female farmers – not to mention the wealth overall accumulated by white America from the labor of African farmers throughout the region.

No narrative of Black farmers and agriculture can be complete without referring to the agriculturalist and scientist, George Washington Carver, who played as extraordinary role through his work at Tuskegee University in Alabama. Many say he saved the South. This is probably true. Carver recognized that the depleted soil from cotton production could be alleviated by a rotation of crops. Cotton, for example, should be rotated with legumes such as peanuts to fix nitrogen in the soil and farmers today are largely attentive to this practice. This example of rotation just touches on his genius but also his teaching model of a "moveable school" was transformative for agriculture education in the South, as in taking education directly to the farmer. This is something the Federation and other institutions have also adapted in many instances whether or not they recognize Carver's role in the development of the model.

Tuskegee agriculture professors will often bring their students to the Federation's Rural Training and Research Center in Epes, Alabama to meet some of the Black farmers in the area. One professor told me that the students can then witness a farmer digging his hand into the soil and tell them precisely about its health or what was needed to improve it. It comes from traditional knowledge, of course, and is beyond the textbook.

Black farmers have also played a central role in the movement for freedom and justice in the United States and are rarely acknowledged for this. In the mid-20th century, across the South, they assisted in funding some civil rights initiatives and worked with students and activists including the Student Non-Violent Coordinating Committee (SNCC); they offered their land on occasion to assist civil rights workers, as in for camping; they ran for positions in USDA agriculture committees, such as the Agricultural Stabilization and Conservation Service (ASCS), which is now the Farm Service Agency (FSA); they assisted in voter registration initiatives. These are just a few examples.

Importantly, the legendary 1965 Voting Rights March from Selma-to-Montgomery on Highway 80 could probably never have occurred were it not for Black farmers. Black farmers, who owned land along Highway 80, allowed the integrated mixture of black and white marchers to stay on their land during the 54-mile march. This would never have been allowed on white-owned farms along the route.

Black farmers are, in fact, at the pinnacle of American heroes in the movement for justice in America and should be acknowledged as such!

As Black farmers were often the levers upon which the movement rested in rural areas, the conservative and reactionary whites in the South went after them with a vengeance that included, of course, the representatives of the U.S. Department of Agriculture.

In his book "Dispossession: Discrimination against African American Farmers in the Age of Civil Rights," historian Pete Daniel describes the USDA and the white south's tactics. Daniel managed to obtain records from the "U.S. Commission on Civil Rights" of studies that were conducted, for one, in 1965 and 1967 and he said that after his years of research, even he was shocked by the tactics to undermine Black farmers. Countless farmers were forced off the land during this period and/or left the South under the circumstances.

Daniel states, for example,

> When SNCC in the mid-1960s organized African American farmers to vote in ASCS elections, county offices issued inaccurate maps, neglected to send black women ballots, manipulated ballots to confuse black farmers, all with the complicity of the Washington USDA office. There was also violence, intimidation, and economic retaliation.

Largely in response to this discrimination, the Federation was created in 1967. It grew out of the civil rights movement. As the late Alabama attorney J.L. Chestnut once said, "There were a lot of organizations that were spawned by the blood that was spilled on the Edmund Pettus Bridge in Selma in 1965, and the Federation was one of those." Elders in the movement have told me that they felt the civil rights movement at the time had left the rural South behind. So the Federation was created to help fill that void by playing a role in saving black-owned land and offering tools for economic development.

As the founders of the Federation were, of course, aware of the discrimination against Black farmers in the South, they created an expansive organization that is licensed in 16 Southern states. It has offered assistance in seeking resources from the USDA for farmers, and, through the cooperative economic development model, provided another significant framework for economic advancement. Its work has also included international outreach and assistance in Cuba, West Africa, the Caribbean and Haiti to name a few. This is often with international farmer-to-farmer exchange programs.

In its more that four decades, the Federation has assisted in the creation of agriculture cooperatives, fisher cooperatives, craft cooperatives, credit unions and other cooperative ventures in addition to an important infrastructure of State Associations of Cooperatives. It has remained a grassroots organization.

In addition to assisting individual Black farmers, the Federation has played a significant role effecting federal policy. In the early 1990s, Congress passed what was known as the "Minority Farmers Rights Act" that would, for the first time, use federal funds for programs targeted for Black farmers. It was proposed by the Federation in 1988. While the bill passed Congress, funds were not appropriated. It took a "Caravan to Washington" in 1992 of farmers and supporters from across the South, to finally pressure Congress to appropriate monies for the program. The "Caravan" was the brainchild of the former executive director, Ralph Paige.

Importantly, the Federation was instrumental in the filing of the Black Farmer Class Action Lawsuit against the USDA that settled in 1999. It was known as the Pigford v Glickman lawsuit with Tim Pigford being a Black farmer from North Carolina and Dan Glickman being President Bill Clinton's Secretary of Agriculture. This was the largest civil rights lawsuit ever filed against the United States government. To date, more than a billion dollars has been allocated to Black farmers for the discrimination they experienced from the USDA.

The above is but a brief summary of the expansive work of the Federation in the Black Belt South. Its important contributions have offered hope and an inspiration to many throughout the region and the world. The Federation and Black farmers have played a significant role in both honoring and saving family farmers for the benefit of farmers themselves and their communities, of course, as well as for all of us in America in providing food, in significant contributions to our culture and the integrity of our communities over all.

Eliminate Hunger and Poverty by Encouraging Family Farming

Danielle Nierenberg

Danielle Nierenberg is president of Food Tank and an expert on food issues. She has written extensively on the topic of sustainable agriculture and factory farming in the developing world.

After decades of failed attempts to eradicate hunger, development agencies, international research institutions, non-profit organizations, and the funding and donor communities now see family farmers as key to alleviating global poverty and hunger. Recent estimates show that currently, 1.2 billion people in the world live in extreme poverty, and at least 870 million go to bed hungry every night. As the world gears up for the International Year of Family Farming in 2014, Food Tank: The Food Think Tank and the U.N. Food and Agriculture Organization (FAO) are highlighting effective ways to provide family farmers with the tools they need to really nourish the world.

FAO's High Level Panel of Experts on Food Security and Nutrition (HLPE) reports that approximately 96 percent of all the agricultural holdings in Africa measure less than ten hectares. FAO Agricultural Census data shows that around 80 percent of agricultural holdings in sub-Saharan Africa and 88 percent of those in developing countries in Asia measure less than 2 hectares.

Family farmers play a crucial role in resolving world hunger, but they're also those most likely to fall victim to hunger and poverty. An estimated 800 million people living below the global poverty line work in the agricultural sector. In China and India alone there are respectively 189 million and 112 million smallholder farmers with plots measuring less than two hectares.

"Family Farming is the Key to Alleviating Hunger and Poverty," by Danielle Nierenberg, Food Tank, October 7, 2013. Reprinted by permission.

And yet, smallholder agriculture has great potential to reduce overall national poverty levels. According to a landmark World Bank report, an increase of one percent in agricultural GDP reduces poverty by four times as much as the same percentage increase in non-agricultural GDP.

Food Tank is working with FAO to highlight the important role that family farmers play in the food system. Over the next two years, both organizations will work to shine a spotlight on how family farming can enhance soil health, protect water supplies, improve nutrition, and increase incomes. Small-scale, family-run farms not only form the base of rural communities in both the developing and developed world and provide a large number of jobs, but they are also at the center of sustainable production.

Small-scale farmers can contribute significantly to the transformation of agriculture by managing land and water responsibly, protect water supplies, preserve and enhance biodiversity, and contribute to climate change adaptation and mitigation. A large study examining smallholder agriculture by the Department of Biological Sciences and Centre for Environment and Society at the University of Essex covered 286 projects, over 37 million hectares in 57 developing countries, and found that when sustainable agriculture was adopted, average crop yields increased by 79 percent.

"By working with family farmers to build on their knowledge in the development of sustainable agricultural practices, we can improve resilience in the food system—including resilience to climate change, food price shocks, conflict, and natural disasters," says Barbara Gemmill-Herren, Programme Officer at FAO.

Food Tank and FAO present five effective ways for NGOs, the funding and donor communities, and policy-makers to invest more effectively in family farming:

Promote Sustainable Agriculture Methods

New farming methods, such as agroecology or ecological intensification, increase yields while reducing environmental impacts. In an analysis of 40 projects and programs, sustainable techniques like agroforestry and soil conservation were found to increase yields for African smallholder farmers. The Cambodian Center for Study and Development in Agriculture (CEDAC) has partnered with Farmer and Nature Net (FNN) to promote the System of Rice Intensification (SRI), which has been shown to increase yields and improve soil fertility while reducing the use of chemicals and maintaining local ownership of seeds.

Assist Family Farmers in Adapting to Climate Change and Short-Term Climate Variability

Climate change will have large-scale effects on agriculture everywhere, and particularly on poor farmers in developing countries. According to IFAD, in Africa alone, because of climate change 75 million to 250 million more people will experience increased water stress by 2020. Year-to-year climate variability in the form of drought or flooding already has large-scale effects on food security today. Throughout sub-Saharan Africa, Farmer Field Schools teaching smallholder farmers sustainable practices in land and water management have proven highly effective in managing input such as pesticides more effectively while increasing yields and incomes.

Promote Policies to Provide Smallholders with Legal Titles to Their Land

At least one billion poor people lack secure rights to land. Securing legal land rights for family farmers can increase productivity, investment in land, and family income. Landesa works with countries to design and implement land rights programs, and has helped 100 million farmers obtain or secure ownership over their land.

Increase Access to Local Markets

The small-scale production volumes of family farmers require value chains of appropriate scale. Farmers markets or Community-

Supported Agriculture (CSA) can provide a great venue for family farmers to sell their products directly to consumers. For example, the organization GrowNYC manages 54 markets in New York, providing a sales channel to 230 farms and fishermen.

Close the Gender Gap

Women farmers do not have the same access to credit, land, inputs, and extension services as their male counterparts. According to FAO, closing the gender gap in agricultural inputs alone could lift 100–150 million people out of hunger. The Latin American and Caribbean Center for Rural Women (Enlac) serves as an organizing voice for marginalized, rural women, calling for equal access to land rights, and, boosting access to clean water, and conserving native seeds.

If public and private sectors direct funding toward family farmers and research that would support them, smallholder agriculture can get the push it needs to nourish both people and the planet.

Family Farms Are Better than Industrial Farms for a Variety of Reasons

Beyond Factory Farming

Beyond Factory Farming (BFF) is an organization based in Canada that promotes responsible, safe, fair, and healthy livestock production.

Have you ever asked yourself "why is sustainable agriculture so much better than industrial agriculture?" The text below should give you a quick and easy comparison of the two types of production methods and the benefit of sustainable meat production should be clear.

Health Issues

Family Farm

- foods are produced without the use of pesticides, hormones, antibiotics, and other hazardous inputs.

Industrial Operation

- overuse of antibiotics leads to antibiotic resistance.
- odours can cause nausea, headaches, and respiratory problems especially to barn workers.[1]
- bacteria and parasites from animal waste which are chlorine resistant and may cause human disease.[2]

Antibiotic (Antimicrobial) Issues

Family Farm

- animals are raised without the routine use of antibiotics.
- antibiotics are only administered to a sick animal.
- organic farmers pull the sick animal from the herd before treating it and the meat is not sold under that label.

"Industrial vs. Family Farms Comparison," Beyond Factory Farming. Reprinted by permission.

Industrial Operation

- routine use of antibiotics is used to promote growth and prevent disease.[3]
- due to crowded and unhealthy conditions routine use of antibiotics in industrial facilities is believed to lead to antibiotic resistance in humans[4] making antibiotics less effective leaving the elderly, medically vulnerable, and children at risk.
- up to 90% of all antibiotics used in livestock production in Canada are not used to treat sick animals but are used as growth promoters.[5]

Environmental Issues

Family Farm

- sustainable farmers recognize the importance of protecting the natural environment and act as stewards of the land.

Industrial Operation

- industrial facilities contribute to numerous environmental issues such as damage to our air, water, and soil.
- overapplication of manure can lead to contamination of water.

Animal Waste Issues

Family Farm

- sustainable farms only raise what the land is capable of handling.
- farmers use manure or composted manure as fertilizer for crops which reduces or eliminates the need for commercial fertilizers and chemicals.

Industrial Operation

- industrial livestock production concentrates large numbers of animals in one area. As a result, there is too much manure concentrated in one area for the land to handle.

- Manure is stored in large holding pits, lagoons, or stock piled.
- Due to high transportation costs, manure is often over-applied to fields close to the operation.
- Manure becomes something factory farms must dispose of instead of a fertilizer.
- liquid manure is often sprayed onto land and crops as raw, untreated sewage.
- such large amounts of manure not only cause excessive odours but they also release hazardous gases into the air and contaminate water sources with pathogens, phosphourous, and nitrogen.
- manure storage emits gases such as ammonia, hydrogen sulfide, and methane. These gases can cause noxious odours, as well as a suite of health problems.[6]

Water Waste Issues

Family Farm

- sustainable farms protect water sources and conserve water.

Industrial Operation

- industrial operations use huge amounts of water for liquefying manure, flushing barns, and drinking water for animals.
- industrial operations often contaminate water sources with excess nutrients, hormone and antibiotic residue, and harmful pathogens.
- livestock manure has up to 30 times more power to pollute surface water than human waste.[7]

Soil Issues

Family Farm

- sustainable farms apply animal manure at a rate that the land can handle protect riparian areas.

Industrial Operation

- excess nitrogen in manure can evaporate as ammonia.[8]
- excess nitrogen and phosphorous left behind can not only alter soil characteristics, and thus productivity, but also run off into nearby streams and rivers and affect water supplies.[9]
- undigested feed may contain trace amounts of heavy metals and salts that accumulate in manure storage units. The accumulated metals may sit in the bottom of storage container for extended periods. When a spill or leak occurs, these metals end up in the soil.
- metals that are often found in manure include copper, zinc, cadmium, molybdenum, nickel, lead, iron, manganese, and boron. If applied to the soil or spilled, high concentrations of heavy metals can reduce the types of crops that will grow in soil.[10]

Hormone Issues

- no hormones are administered to animals on sustainable farms.

Industrial Operation

- 3 natural hormones and 3 synthetic hormones have been approved for use in beef in Canada.[11]
- hormones are used to achieve leaner beef, increase in growth using less feed, and to reduce the cost for producers.[12]
- consumption of hormone-treated beef may cause girls to reach puberty earlier, thus making them more susceptible to breast and other cancers.[13]

Genetic Diversity Issues

Family Farm

- sustainable farms help preserve genetic diversity by raising a wide range of animal breeds.
- many of these breeds are chosen due to the geographic areas in which they are raised.

Industrial Operation

- Industrial farms reduce genetic diversity in animals because they only raise a few selected breeds.
- the need for quick growth and high output requires genetic qualities that provide a more uniform product.

Fuel Issues

Family Farm

- sustainable farms use efficient application of manure and crop rotation to minimize fuel consumption.

Industrial Operation

- intensive livestock production contributes 80% of agriculture's greenhouse gas emissions.[14]

Transportation Issues

Family Farm

- sustainable farms sell their product locally through farmer's markets, local stores, or community supported agriculture (CSA) programs. This prevents environmental damage and human health problems caused by transportation-generated pollution.

Industrial Operation

- industrial-scale livestock production is usually centralized and therefore requires extensive transportation.
- as the distance food travels increases, so does the role of chemicals and processing to reduce spoilage before the food reaches the marketplace.[15]
- food animals often travel many hours without food or water.[16]

Animal Welfare Issues

Family Farm

- Sustainably-raised animals are treated humanely and are permitted to carry out natural behaviours such as rooting in the dirt and pecking the ground.

Industrial Operation

- industrial animals are crammed together in confined areas or cages without access to sunlight, fresh air, or open pasture.
- Densely populated confinement barns limit animal movement and increase the potential for rapid spread of disease.[17]
- many undergo painful mutilations such as castration, tail-docking and branding without anesthesia or pain relief.[18]
- most food animals are forced to endure the agony of long-distance transport. Current federal legislation stipulates that it's legal to transport food animals anywhere from 36 to 52 hours (depending on the species) without water, food or a rest stop.[19]

Economic/Community Issues

Family Farm

- sustainable farms support local economies by purchasing supplies and materials from local businesses.
- Owners of small, sustainable farms are actively involved in their communities, helping to build resilient rural communities.

Industrial Operation

- many communities are left with the cost of environmental damage.[20]
- negative impacts on a community both socially and economically outweigh any positive.

- industrial livestock facilities hire as few workers as possible and typically purchase equipment, supplies, and animal feed from companies outside the area.[21]
- small rural communities are divided when industrial livestock facilities are located in rural areas.

Worker Issues

Family Farm

- sustainable farm owners provide a safe working environment.

Industrial Operation

- workers are inside the barn where air quality is at its worst.
- Among the most serious hazards faced by workers is routine exposure to dust and gases emitted from sources of concentrated manure.
- they are subjected to an array of hazards such as respiratory infections, sprains, bruises, severe head trauma, fractures, electrocution and repetitive motion injury.[22]

Footnotes

1. Intensive Livestock Operations and Health Problems, Paul Hasselback, Encompass, volume 2, no. 2, December 1997

2. "Agricultural antibiotics and resistance in human pathogens: villain or scapegoat?" Allison J. McGeer, Msc MD, Canadian Medical Association Journal, Nov. 3, 1998

3. Antibiotic Resistant Factories factsheet, Cathy Holtslander, Beyond Factory Farming Coalition, 2007

4. "Agricultural use of antibiotics and the evolution and transfer of antibiotic-resistant bacteria", George G. Khachatoruians, BA, MA, PhD, Canadian Medical Association Journal, Nov. 3, 1998

5. It's Hitting the Fan, Environmental Defence Canada, 2002

6. ibid.

7. ibid.

8. ibid.

9. ibid.

10. "Understanding Hormone Use in Beef", Canadian Cattlemen's Association and Beef Information Centre, February 2006

11. ibid.

12. "The Real Dope on Beef", Bradford Duplisea, Canadian Health Coalition, (Calgary Herald), 2001

13. ibid.

14. Livestock's long shadow, Environmental issues and options, H. Steinfeld, P. Gerber, T. Wassenaar, V. Castel, M. Rosales, C. deHann, 2006

15. "Food Miles", http://www.sierraclub.ca, Sierra Club of Canada 16. Inching toward humane treatment for food animals, Lynn Kavanaugh, The Vancouver Sun, June 14, 2007

17. It's Hitting the Fan, Environmental Defence Canada, 2002

18. Inching toward humane treatment for food animals, Lynn Kavanaugh, The Vancouver Sun, June 14, 2007

19. ibid.

20. Large-Scale Hog Production and Processing: Concerns for Manitobans, Commissioners' Report on the Citizens' Hearing on Hog Production and the Environment, Brandon, Manitoba, October 1999

21. Pollution Shopping in Rural America: The myth of economic development in isolated regions, Dr. William J. Weida, March 2001

22. Intensive Livestock Operations and Your Health, http://www.sierraclub.ca, Sierra Club of Canada

CHAPTER 3

Should There Be More Government Regulation and Intervention in Agriculture?

Governmental Regulation of Agriculture

John Freebairn

John Freebairn is a professor of economics at the University of Melbourne. One of Freebairn's specialties is environmental economics.

The Productivity Commission's latest draft report on the regulation of agriculture highlights the need to get the balance right, as to when the government should and shouldn't intervene in this industry, and then how to intervene.

The report is part of a nine-month public inquiry into the regulatory burden on farm businesses. It covers a wide range of issues from land and water use to labour and foreign investment.

Agriculture is fairly unique in that market competition is pervasive. Competitive markets provide the incentives and rewards for businesses to find cost-effective production methods, develop new products valued by buyers, and to adopt technology. At the same time, agriculture has to compete against alternative uses of limited national natural resources, labour and capital, and the sector has to pay market rates for these inputs.

Markets work well only with well-defined property rights, ranging from weights and measures for the products produced, through to the rights and responsibilities of owners in the use of land, water, labour, transport infrastructure, and other key inputs. Here, the Productivity Commission's report questions current regulations on some property rights. For example, they restrict decisions on the potential use of land for agriculture versus for the environment, urban use and mining, and they restrict the opportunities for non-resident investment in agriculture much more than investment in mining and manufacturing.

The commission proposes that regulations should balance the opportunity costs of alternative uses of land, or restrictions on the use of land. For example, the value of land regulated for use for agriculture should be compared with the value to society if instead the land was restricted to the provision of the environment, mining or urban growth.

It also proposes the government intervene to correct market failures. This could include for example the effects of the exercise of market power, external costs and lack of information necessary for buyers and sellers to make informed decisions.

Examples of external costs include run-off of chemicals to rivers and the ocean, irrigation in some areas increasing salinity downstream, and biosecurity. Often Australian food markets do not provide buyers with required information about the production systems used, for example organic or GMO, about food safety and nutrition.

As the Productivity Commission notes, regulation is not the only form of government intervention and often it is not the best way to correct a market failure. For example, the creation of government environmental water managers with water property rights similar to those used by irrigators for the Murray-Darling Basin seems to be a more effective way to restore a balance of water use between irrigation and the environment, than previous restrictions on water available for irrigation.

Sometimes government failure, either from lack of information or the dominance of political considerations, can result in regulations with larger social costs than those for the market failure. Essentially this is reflected in the report's argument that some regulations are counter productive, such as the banning of GMO and regulation the sugar industry again.

Where regulation is a proposed solution to the market failure, a next step is to design the regulation. The objective is to balance the benefits and costs to society, and not just for agriculture, of the restrictions imposed on the products produced and the production methods used.

In many cases these social benefit cost assessments will be very challenging and with legitimate debates on key costs and benefits. Regulations on animal welfare illustrate. There are challenges in providing robust measures of animal welfare and even in obtaining estimates of the different values and attitudes people place on different levels of animal welfare.

Forthcoming information about the side effects of new chemicals and production methods, as well as the evolution of society preferences, likely will justify adapting and changing regulations over time as new information becomes available.

A particular area of excessive regulation cost affecting Australian agriculture identified by the Productivity Commission concerns over-lapping, and sometimes conflicting, regulations across the three levels of government.

Greater inter-government cooperation over the design and conduct of regulations is what the Productivity Commission draft report proposes and the government would do well to listen.

GMOs Need to Be Regulated

Dana Perls

Dana Perls is involved with the worldwide environmental group Friends of the Earth.

"The apple that never browns wants to change your mind about genetically modified foods."

That headline in the Washington Post is just one of many shining the spotlight on the next generation of genetically modified organisms (what many are calling GMO 2.0) heading to our supermarkets and restaurants.

Gene-silenced Arctic apples that do not turn brown when exposed to air, even when rotten, will be sold in stores in the Midwest this week. Other products on the way include canola oil extracted from rapeseed that has been modified by gene editing to withstand more pesticides, but which is being marketed as a non-GMO food by its maker; salmon genetically engineered with eel genes to grow faster; and synthetic vanillin excreted from genetically modified yeast, yet marketed as "natural."

Researchers are tinkering with nature's DNA in new and potentially problematic ways and without clear regulatory guidance. They can alter a species by editing or deleting genes, turning genes on or off, or even creating completely new DNA sequences on a computer. Some of these new foods will be marketed as "non-GMO" or "natural" because the definition of GMO has not yet caught up with the pace of new biotechnology developments.

Existing definitions focus on *transgenic* technologies that take genes from one species and put them into another. But many companies are modifying organisms' genomes without adding another organisms's genes using gene-silencing techniques such as RNA interference and gene-editing techniques such as CRISPR.

"Next-generation genetically modified foods need better regulation," by Dana Perls, STAT, February 2, 2017. Reprinted by permission.

New GMO foods are being released with little understanding of their potential health and environmental consequences. So far, no safety assessments specific to these new techniques are required, and no regulatory oversight is in place for this swiftly moving set of new technologies.

To address that gap in regulations, the Department of Agriculture recently announced a proposal for updating its biotechnology regulations. While it is good that the USDA is considering regulating gene-edited foods, the proposal is riddled with loopholes that could exclude many new GMO foods. I believe that *all* genetically engineered crops, including ones made with gene-editing tools like CRISPR, should be regulated and assessed for health and environmental impacts.

Biotech companies in this emerging market hope consumers are attracted to new GMO products. Intrexon, the company that makes the non-browning GMO Arctic apple, believes that this product may lead to less food waste. Yet there's a reason an apple turns brown—it's a signal it has been cut or bruised. If a little oxidizing is worrisome, we can use lemon juice, a proven, natural method to prevent it. Some scientists believe apples' natural browning enzyme may help fight diseases and pests, meaning that farmers may have to increase their pesticide use to grow non-browning apples.

Research also suggests that newer technologies such as gene silencing may pose health risks, and some of the genetic material used, such as double-stranded RNA, could affect gene expression in human cells in ways that have not yet been investigated.

The first generation of GMOs was promoted to reduce pesticide use in agriculture. Yet data show that the widespread use of GMO crops has actually *increased* the use of glyphosate-based Roundup herbicide. Not only are there serious environmental consequences associated with such an increase, but the International Agency for Research on Cancer recently declared that glyphosate is a probable human carcinogen, and a recent long-term study linked low doses of Roundup to serious liver damage.

We understand even less about the potential unintended impacts of GMO 2.0 foods. It is unclear how these new technologies might evolve once released into the environment; how they might interact with their ecosystems; and whether they might result in permanent changes to other organisms or ecosystems.

Although some experts suggest that gene-editing techniques like CRISPR are more precise than the first-generation genetic engineering technologies, there are still documented off-target effects, meaning they will likely have unintended consequences. CRISPR will probably be used to produce more herbicide-tolerant GMOs, which will perpetuate the toxic treadmill of increased chemical dependency in agriculture, taking us further away from healthy food systems.

There are also serious sustainability concerns with GMO 2.0 foods. For example, using genetically modified yeast to make vanillin requires vast amounts of feedstock — the sugary broth used to grow yeast. Common feedstocks, usually from corn or sugar cane, are typically produced in chemical-intensive industrial agricultural systems.

GMO 2.0 foods could also affect millions of small sustainable farmers around the world whose livelihoods depend on growing the valuable natural crops that will be replaced. Many synthetic biology products are intended to replace plant-based commodities typically grown in developing countries, such as vanilla, saffron, cacao, coconut, shea butter, stevia, and others. This raises serious questions about who will benefit from the production of these new technologies and who will bear the costs. A holistic analysis of sustainability—which hasn't yet been done—would likely point to the many environmental and social shortcomings of this next generation of biotechnologies.

Fortunately, food companies and retailers are listening to consumer demand. Fast food companies like McDonald's and Wendy's have said they will not carry the GMO apple. More than 60 major grocery stores, including Walmart, Costco, Albertsons, and others, have committed not to carry the GMO salmon.

The Non-GMO Project and the National Organic Standards Board have made it clear that GMO 2.0 technologies like gene silencing and CRISPR are, indeed, genetic engineering techniques that must not be used in the production and manufacture of any product carrying the Non-GMO Verified or USDA Organic labels. Now it's time for the US government to add its voice to the issue. We need more science, assessment, answers, and regulations before we can decide whether these new biotech products should be in our stores—and on our plates. Instead, we are being kept in the dark, with no clue about what foods contain these unlabeled ingredients.

There is widespread consumer concern about GMOs and genetically modified foods. Friends of the Earth is working with various allies to educate the public about the next generation of GMOs. Instead of being swayed by Intrexon's narrative of the value of non-browning GMO Arctic apples, we want food that is truly natural, sustainable, organic, and healthy.

Inspection of Food and Regulation of Pesticides

United States Environmental Protection Agency

The US Environmental Protection Agency (EPA) is a governmental agency. It oversees a wide range of environmental issues important to the well-being of US citizens.

Pesticides are widely used in producing food to control pests such as insects, rodents, weeds, bacteria, mold and fungus.

Under the Food Quality Protection Act (FQPA), EPA must ensure that all pesticides used on food in the United States meet FQPA's stringent safety standard. FQPA requires an explicit determination that a pesticide's use on food is safe for children and includes an additional safety factor, tenfold unless data show a different factor to be protective, to account for uncertainty in data relative to children.

The science and our understanding of chemical risk evolves and EPA continues to reevaluate each pesticide's safety every 15 years. EPA's continuous reevaluation of registered pesticides, combined with strict FQPA standards, major improvements in science, and an increase in the use of safer, less toxic pesticides, has led to an overall trend of reduced risk from pesticides.

Is Food Grown Using Pesticides Safe to Eat?

EPA is confident that the fruits and vegetables our children are eating are safer than ever. Under FQPA, EPA evaluates new and existing pesticides to ensure that they can be used with a reasonable certainty of no harm to infants and children as well as adults. EPA works continually to review and improve safety standards that apply to pesticide residues on food.

It is important to note though, that just because a pesticide residue is detected on a fruit or vegetable, that does not mean it is

"Food and Pesticides," United States Environmental Protection Agency, March 6, 2019.

unsafe. Very small amounts of pesticides that may remain in or on fruits, vegetables, grains, and other foods decrease considerably as crops are harvested, transported, exposed to light, washed, prepared and cooked. The presence of a detectible pesticide residue does not mean the residue is at an unsafe level. USDA's Pesticide Data Program (PDP) detects residues at levels far lower than those that are considered health risks.

What Has EPA Done to Decrease or Restrict the Amount of Pesticides In Food?

The 1996 FQPA directed EPA to completely reassess pesticide residues on food, with a special emphasis on the unique vulnerability of children. From 1996 to 2006, EPA used the improved safety standards in FQPA to cancel or restrict the use of 270 pesticides for household and food uses because they posed particular threats to children and infants. EPA also lowered the permissible pesticide residue levels for many kid's foods—for example, apples, grapes, and potatoes.

The FQPA safety standard isn't the only reason why EPA has been able to take so many steps to reduce children's exposure to pesticides in recent years. Once a pesticide is registered for its specific uses, it is not left unchecked. Starting in 2007, EPA began the systematic reevaluation of all old pesticides.

Here are some notable EPA actions:

- In 2009, EPA canceled all uses of carbofuran, canceled aldicarb use on potatoes and citrus, and canceled methamidophos use on all commodities.
- In 2010, EPA canceled methomyl use on grapes and strawberries.
- In 2010, EPA canceled all products containing methyl parathion.
- In 2012 EPA canceled acephate use on green beans, oxamyl use on soybeans, and imidacloprid use on almonds.

- In 2013, EPA canceled all domestic uses of methyl parathion and canceled all uses of formetanate HCI on apples, pears, and peaches.

We have seen, through USDA's Pesticide Data Program (PDP) data, an overall decrease in the amount of pesticide residues in food, especially since the passing of FQPA in 1996. The stricter standards of FQPA and major improvements in science and data, and an increase in the use of safer, less toxic pesticides, has led to an overall trend of reduced risk from pesticides.

For example, from 1995 to 2013, children's exposure to carbamates (a group of insecticides that affect the nervous system) fell by 70%—EPA canceled or restricted many carbamates during this time. From 1998 to 2008, tomatoes with detectable organophosphate pesticide residues fell from 37% to 9%, due to EPA canceling most organophosphates. It is important to note for some of the more recent actions, EPA expects declines will show up in future PDP data.

How Does EPA Regulate Pesticides In Food?

EPA evaluates every new pesticide and every new use for safety before registration. Before they may be sold, EPA must ensure that pesticides are safe for human health and the environment when used according to label directions. For each pesticide, EPA evaluates hundreds of different scientific studies.

Through these evaluations, EPA is ensuring the overall safety of proposed pesticide uses as required by FQPA. After pesticide registration, EPA reevaluates its safety every 15 years, taking into consideration any new data.

EPA's process for registering and re-evaluating pesticides is not a closed-door process between EPA and pesticide manufacturers. EPA relies on the best science available and places high value on transparency in decision-making. The public is invited to comment throughout the decision-making process—we request studies and data, take our findings to independent expert panels such as the FIFRA Scientific Advisory Panel, and consult the National Academy of Sciences on broad scientific policy questions. The agency also frequently receive hundreds or even thousands of comments from the public on our draft assessments and proposed decisions.

Public concerns about specific pesticides and food safety do not go unnoticed at EPA. We take incidents of pesticide poisoning and exposure very seriously and look at those incidents as part of our review. EPA can and has used its authority to have products removed from the market immediately when risks are imminent.

At the same time that we review dietary exposure to pesticides, we also look at worker exposure and environmental exposure. Risks to workers and the environment can lead to cancelations as well, or restrictions on how and when a pesticide can be used, including, when appropriate, establishing 'no spray' buffer zones to protect the surrounding communities and waterways.

Before allowing the use of a pesticide on food crops, EPA sets a maximum legal residue limit (called a tolerance) for each treated food. The tolerance is the residue level that triggers enforcement action. That is, if residues are found above that level, the commodity will be subject to seizure by the government. EPA receives information on how much pesticide residue remains on various foods through the PDP. Through annual sampling, PDP has collected thousands of samples on 10-15 food commodities and can detect residues at levels far lower than those that that pose health risks.

In setting the tolerance, EPA must make a safety finding that the pesticide can be used with "reasonable certainty of no harm." To make this finding, EPA considers the toxicity of the pesticide and its breakdown products, how much of the pesticide is applied and how often, and how much of the pesticide (i.e., the residue) remains in or on food by the time it is marketed. EPA ensures that the tolerance selected will be safe. The tolerance applies to food grown in the U.S. and imported food.

Inequality Is Common in the US Agricultural System and Must Be Countered

Megan Horst

Megan Horst is an assistant professor at Portland State University in Urban Studies and Planning, where she also chairs the Diversity and Equity Committee.

Farming in the United States is enmeshed with both racism and capitalism in a way that has had a profound impact on who owns, accesses, and benefits from farmland. Recently, I published research with Portland State University student Amy Marion examining data on non-farming landowners, farmers who own and lease land, and farmworkers. We found significant racial/ethnic disparities when it comes to representation, land, and money.

Perhaps not surprisingly to those familiar with structural racism in the food system, we found that white Americans are most likely to own land and benefit from the wealth it generates. From 2012 to 2014, white people comprised over 97 percent of non-farming landowners, 96 percent of owner-operators, and 86 percent of tenant operators. They also generated 98 percent of all farm-related income from land ownership and 97 percent of the income that comes from operating farms.

On the other hand, farmers of color (Black, Asian, Native American, Pacific Islander, and those reporting more than one race) comprised less than 3 percent of non-farming landowners and less than 4 percent of owner-operators. They were more likely to be tenants than owners; they also owned less land and smaller farms, and generated less wealth from farming than their white counterparts.

"New Research Explores the Ongoing Impact of Racism on the U.S. Farming Landscape," by Megan Horst, Civil Eats, January 25, 2019. This story was originally published by Civil Eats, an online daily news site focused on the American Food System and republished with permission.

Meanwhile, Latin farmers comprised about 2 percent of non-farming landowners and about 6 percent of owner-operators and tenant operators, well below their 17 percent representation in the U.S. population. They also comprised over 80 percent of farm laborers, a notoriously under-compensated, difficult, and vulnerable position in U.S. farming.

In other words, despite greater diversity in the U.S. population overall and seeming progress in other areas of racial equity, farming in this country appears to be as segregated as it was a century ago. Inequity is part of American farming history, with few exceptions.

Structural Racism and US Agriculture

One exceptional moment occurred in the decades after the Civil War, when freed slaves and their descendants accumulated 19 million acres of land. In 1910, 14 percent of all farm owner-operators were Black or African Americans. By 2012, however, they comprised only 1.5 percent.

The causes of that decline, and today's disparities, are rooted in the structural racism that has been part and parcel of the development of modern U.S. agriculture. Not only were Native Americans often violently removed from their homelands (which were further segmented by federal laws), but a series of federal Homestead Acts gave mainly white male settlers and corporations hugely subsidized land.

Discriminatory laws, such as the California Alien Land Law of 1913, prohibited various people of color from owning land. They were also denied reparations after the abolition of slavery, as well as labor protections like minimum wage, union rights, and social security when they worked on farms. The government gave unequal funding to land-grant universities that served Black and white students, and the U.S. Department of Agriculture (USDA) discriminated against Black, Native American, Latin, and women farmers in its lending and other forms of support for decades.

Together, this legacy has had profound and lasting impacts to the U.S. food system. As farmer Leah Penniman pointed out recently, "If African-American people [had been] paid $20 per week for our agricultural labor rather than being enslaved, we would have trillions in the bank today."

But that obviously didn't happen. Nor were Native Americans appropriately compensated for their land. Instead, the Homestead Acts, which scholar Keri Leigh Merrit calls "unquestionably the most extensive, radical, redistributive governmental policy in U.S. history," had lasting benefits for white people. The National Park Service estimates that about 93 million people, or more than *a quarter of the U.S. adult population*, are descendants of people who received land through the Homestead Acts. That number likely includes a number of today's white farmers and landowners.

More recently, U.S. policy supporting industrialization and consolidation in food production has perpetuated racial and ethnic inequities in more subtle ways. Hundreds of millions in commodity subsidies set aside in the farm bill, technology advances, trademarked plant and animal varieties, and access to international markets has accrued to the largest farms (which are much more likely to be white-owned).

Meanwhile, farmers of color, immigrant farmers, and female farmers, who typically have smaller farms and grow higher-value, labor-intensive products such as fruits, nuts, and vegetables have received less government support. The 2018 Farm Bill continues past trends by offering some important support for diverse farmers, but falling short of structurally transforming the U.S. food system.

Farmers of color face other challenges as well, from challenges in succession planning and a lack of capital to pay taxes and liens, to resistance to farming rooted in the historical trauma associated with slavery. And while interest by young and beginning farmers of diverse races and ethnicities seems to be growing, they start out from a disadvantage, often lacking access to family land or wealth.

This doesn't mean all white farmers have had it easy, either. Many have been pushed out of farming in recent decades due to increasing industrialization and consolidation, which has made American agriculture extremely efficient in some ways, and entirely inhumane and ecologically irresponsible in others. At the same time, agri-businesses get bigger and richer.

Most farmers in America today are struggling. Farmers comprise around 1.5 percent of the population, a percentage that continues to trend downward as young people see little opportunity to make a living. Farmers with differing approaches, farm sizes, and markets are facing stagnant prices, rising costs, difficulties finding labor, and mounting debts. In desperation, farmers are dying by suicide at an alarming rate. And while some food movement activities point to local, direct-to-market farming and organic, sustainable food production as more profitable, plenty of those farmers face hardships, too.

Meanwhile, in a market where the price of land often far exceeds the value that can be made from it for ecological food production, land owners face mounting pressure to sell to developers, oil and gas extraction companies, larger corporate farms, and investment companies. Now, an unprecedented generational transfer of land looms. Over two-thirds of farmland owners are nearing retirement age, and many of them lack clear succession plans. Without a change in direction, the future of farming as a profession held by a diverse group of people is looking pretty bleak.

What's Working and What's Still Needed

There are plenty of inspiring efforts to prioritize diversity and equity in farming. Across the United States, organizations such as Soul Fire Farm in New York state, Mudbone Grown Farm in Portland, Oregon, and the Agriculture and Land-Based Training Association (ALBA) in Salinas, California, provide culturally relevant training and mentoring for new generations of diverse farmers and food cultivators. In the Southeast, Family Agriculture Resource Management Services (FARMS) is providing legal assistance to Black farmers, and all farmers from historically disadvantaged groups, to retain ownership of their land.

But there is still much to be done, and many ways for people and institutions to work for progress in farming equity. White landowners can engage in person-to-person reparations, for example, by paying a land tax to indigenous groups, such as the Shuumi Land Tax that supports returning Chochenyo and Karkin Ohlone lands in the San Francisco Bay Area to indigenous stewardship.

Other options for white landowners and beneficiaries of white supremacy are to donate land, vehicles, farm equipment, or houses, or share their expertise with farmers of color. Individual actions are not a replacement for a more systematic nation-wide approach, but they can be a step to building a practice and the potential for positive change.

White-led and white-dominated food organizations, from food policy councils to incubator farms, can also reflect on how their practices perpetuate racial privilege. They can go beyond asking how to bring more diverse people to their tables, and instead figure out how to amplify and act in solidarity with existing efforts.

Agricultural institutions, including land grant universities, can confront their racist legacies and build thoughtful and long-term, mutually beneficial relationships with diverse community partners. Grant makers can apply a racial equity lens to their funding decisions. Public agencies and land managers, such as parks departments, can permanently protect land for food cultivation by POC-led organizations.

Building on the example of the Portland Metro, they can also collaborate with Native Americans to make land accessible to hunting, gathering and reclaiming Native foodways.

Activists and organizers can continue to call for racial justice to be acknowledged in the federal farm bill, to combat the massive consolidation and industrialization in farming, to include land and food justice in the Green New Deal, and to call on the federal government to develop proposals for reparations to Native Americans and African Americans.

As researchers, we also call for more attention to the demographics of farmland ownership, farming, and farm labor, and for activist scholarship to help identify emerging best practices in a more equitable U.S. food system.

Ultimately, equitable land access is just part of the vision. Farmers and food producers of all races also need to be able to sustain themselves and their communities. What's needed is no less than a radical transformation of the entire U.S. food system to one that values the people who tend the land and cultivate the food we eat.

Developing Countries and Small Farms Are a Winning Combination

Rachel Wynberg and Laura Pereira

Rachel Wynberg is an associate professor at the University of Cape Town and Laura Pereira is a researcher and lecturer at Stellenbosch University.

Industrial agriculture—farming that involves the intensive production of livestock, poultry, fish and crops—is one of the most environmentally destructive forms of land use. It depends on mechanisation and on inputs like synthetic fertiliser and harmful pesticides and herbicides and has led to widespread contamination of soil and water. It also relies on just a few major crops like wheat, maize, soybean and rice, the seeds of which are owned by a mere handful of companies.

A different approach to agriculture is sorely needed. This should, ideally, deliver household food security, ensure sustainable livelihoods and produce quality nutrition in a rapidly changing climate.

Developing countries that are industrialising at a pace are uniquely placed to avoid developing a dependency on one type of technological innovation at the expense of others. This is what is known as technological lock-in, with industrial agriculture being one form of lock-in. Such countries are also well placed to establish alternative ways to grow food that maximise livelihoods and sustainable food production.

For instance, Brazil, India, China and South Africa have agricultural sectors that have both industrialised farmers and resource-poor farmers who practice low-input agriculture. These countries offer important spaces for strengthening practices that are well suited to the challenges facing smallholder farmers. And ones that are more environmentally sound.

A change in these countries could pioneer alternative approaches for other developing countries.

The basis for alternative agricultural systems already exists. They're practised by at least 75% of the world's 1.5 billion smallholders, family farmers and indigenous peoples.

These alternatives fall broadly under the umbrella of agroecology. Their key characteristics include the use of technologies based on ecological knowledge, as well as a focus on family farming and local production. They also have low levels of external inputs, and are diversified.

Developing countries could leapfrog industrial agriculture systems and move toward an agricultural sector that's run on agroecological principles. But this needs increased public investment and a policy environment that's conducive to encouraging the approach.

Millions Are Doing It Already

Agroecology is already practised by millions of small-scale farmers across the world. China and India, for example, account for 35% and 24% of the world's 570 million family farms. In Brazil, 78% of farms are less than 50 hectares. In South Africa there are about four million small-scale and mostly subsistence farmers.

These farms play a critical role in food security. This is especially true at a local level. But these farmers also face numerous challenges: access to land and capital, secure land rights, appropriate extension and advice, increased climate variability and market access.

The question is whether public money in emerging economies is being used to address these challenges and the needs of small farmers. Or is it being used to prop up large-scale industrial agriculture?

Many emerging economies have dual forms of agriculture—both industrialised and small-scale. Yet investment in agricultural innovations typically centre only on priorities for industrialised farming.

Genetic engineering is an example. It has become one of the main areas of focus in agricultural research over the past three decades. Highly specialised—it involves the modification of an organism by manipulating its genes—it needs high levels of investment. Those developing it also expect high returns and it's very much a "top-down" approach, removed from the context and knowledge of most of the world's farmers, and often bringing questionable benefits.

Solutions

Smallholder agriculture is increasingly important in emerging economies. There is a need for alternative agricultural solutions. Emerging economies can be leaders in this field.

Agroecology presents a tested and forward-looking approach. But it needs to be institutionalised in the allocation of research funding and in science and technology policy.

Agricultural research and development is already playing an important role. Over the past decade there have been increased investments by emerging economies in agricultural research. For example Chinese government investment in agricultural research doubled from 2001 to 2008, exceeding any country except the US. Brazil similarly increased agricultural research and development spending by 46% between 2006 and 2013. South Africa's investment level is more erratic. But it's still high compared to most other sub-Saharan countries.

More needs to be done. Additional steps should include:

- Increased cooperation in agricultural research between countries with large public sector institutes like Brazil and China, and countries with less research capacity, such as Mozambique and Malawi;
- Demonstrating the validity and economic potential of agro-ecology. This can be achieved by drawing on farmers' knowledge, developed over centuries of experimentation; and

- Redesigning formal training and extension programmes to incorporate local knowledge and have a stronger uptake of agroecology in places where resources are scarce.

Emerging economies provide an important opportunity to upscale agroecological innovations to help improve the livelihoods of small and resource-poor farmers and address environmental problems. But they need public investment and an enabling environment to flourish.

Family Farms Are Being Overtaken by Corporate Farming Due to Unfair Regulatory Practices

Chris McGreal

Chris McGreal writes for the Guardian US *and is author of* American Overdose, The Opioid Tragedy in Three Acts.

W hen the vast expanse of rural Iowa was carved up for settlers in the 19th century, it was often divided into 160-acre lots. Four farms made a square mile, with a crisscross of dead-straight roads marking the boundaries like a sprawling chess board.

Within each square, generations of families tended pigs and cattle, grew oats and raised children, with the sons most likely to take over the farm. That is how Barb Kalbach saw the future when she left her family's land to marry and begin farming with her new husband, Jim, 47 years ago.

"When we very first were married, we had cattle and calves," she says. "We raised hogs from farrow to finish, and we had corn, beans, hay and oats. So did everyone around us."

Half a century later, Kalbach surveys the destruction within the section of chessboard she shared with other farms near Dexter in southwestern Iowa. Barb and Jim are the last family still working the land, after their neighbours were picked off by waves of collapsing commodity prices and the rise of factory farming. With that came a vast transfer in wealth as farm profits funnelled into corporations or the diminishing number of families that own an increasing share of the land. Rural communities have been hollowed out.

And while the Kalbachs have hung on to their farm, they long ago abandoned livestock and mixed arable farming for the only thing they can make money at any more—growing corn and soya beans to sell to corporate buyers as feed for animals crammed

"How America's food giants swallowed the family farms," by Chris McGreal, Guardian News and Media Limited, March 9, 2019. Reprinted by permission.

by the thousands into the huge semi-automated sheds that now dominate farming, and the landscape, in large parts of Iowa.

Kalbach comes from five generations of farmers and suspects she may be the last. As she drives the roads around her farmhouse, she ticks off the disappearances.

"That's the Shoesmiths' place," she said. "Two years ago, it had cattle, pigs and pasture."

Now the land is rented out and is all given over to corn. A little further along, the Watts family's farmhouse stands empty, its roof falling in. There are a few relics of the old farm at the place that used to be owned by the Williamses—an abandoned hen house and a bit of machinery—but the land is all corn and soya beans. The Denning house, on Walnut Avenue, was bulldozed after the land was sold and rolled into a bigger operation.

It's a story replicated across America's midwest, with the rapid expansion of farming methods at the heart of the row over US attempts to erode Britain's food standards and lever open access to the UK market as part of a post-Brexit trade deal. Last weekend, the US ambassador to Britain, Woody Johnson, appealed to the UK to embrace US farming, arguing that those who warned against practices such as washing chicken in chlorine had been "deployed" to cast it "in the worst possible light."

His message was greeted with anger by campaigners. Nick Dearden of Global Justice Now warned: "It is really an animal welfare issue here. If UK farmers want to compete against American imports, they will have to lower their standards or go out of business." His words would come as no surprise to Rosemary Partridge, who farms in Sac County, western Iowa. She grew up on an Iowa family farm and then moved with her husband in the late 1970s to raise pigs and grow crops.

"In the past 20 years, where I am, independent hog farming just silently disappeared as the corporates came in," says Partridge. "I live on a hilltop. I can see seven farm families, people my kids went to school with. They're all gone now. My county has 11 small towns, and it's almost like I could look back in slow motion and just see the businesses change and disappear. We've become poorer. Our communities are basically shattered and in more than just an economic way—in a social way too."

This collapse has in good part been driven by the rise of concentrated animal feeding operations, or Cafos. In these industrial farming units, pigs, cows and chickens are crammed by the thousand into rows of barns. Many units are semi-automated, with feeding run by computer and the animals watched by video, with periodic visits by workers who drive between several operations.

"That's how I end up with 40,000 hogs around me," says Partridge.

Cafos account for only a small proportion of America's 2 million farms, but they dominate animal production and have an outsize influence on crop growing, particularly in the midwest.

By one calculation, the US has around 250,000 factory farms of one kind or another. They have their roots in the 1930s, with the mechanisation of pig slaughterhouses. By the 1950s, chickens were routinely packed into huge sheds, in appalling conditions.

In the early 1970s, US agriculture secretary Earl Butz pushed the idea of large-scale farming with the mantra "get big or get out". He wanted to see farmers embrace what he regarded as a more efficient strategy of growing commodity crops, such as corn and soya beans. Some farmers invested heavily in buying land and new machinery to increase production—taking on large amounts of debt to do so.

A decade later, the farm crisis hit as overproduction, the US grain embargo against the Soviet Union and high interest rates dramatically drove up costs and debt for family farms. Land prices collapsed and foreclosures escalated. "Every blow to independent farming made it more of an opportunity for large corporations to come in," said Partridge.

In 1990, small and medium-sized farms accounted for nearly half of all agricultural production in the US. Now it is less than a quarter.

As the medium-sized family farms retreated, the businesses they helped support disappeared. Local seed and equipment suppliers shut up shop because corporations went straight to wholesalers or manufacturers. Demand for local vets collapsed. As those businesses packed up and left, communities shrank. Shops, restaurants and doctors' surgeries closed. People found they had to drive for an hour or more for medical treatment. Towns and counties began to share ambulances.

Corporate agriculture evolved to take control of the entire production line from "farm to fork," from the genetics of breeding to wholesalers in the US or far east. As factory farms spread, their demands dictated the workings of slaughterhouses. Smaller abattoirs, which offered choice and competitive prices to family farmers, disappeared, to be replaced by huge operations that were further away and imposed lower prices on small-scale breeders such as the Kalbachs.

"By the time you paid to transport them the extra distance, and they were paying you less than they paid the corporations because you weren't bringing the big numbers, there was really no money in it," says Kalbach.

The buying power of the Cafos also helps drive farmers' decisions on which crops to grow. With no livestock, the Kalbachs were forced into gowing corn and soya beans to sell to factory farms as animal feed or to corporations for ethanol.

Iowa is not alone. Missouri, to the south, had 23,000 independent pig farmers in 1985. Today it has just over 2,000. The number of independent cattle farms has fallen by 40% over the same period.

Tim Gibbons of Missouri Rural Crisis Center, a support group for family farmers set up during the 1980s farm crisis, says the cycle of economic shocks has blended with government policies to create a "monopolisation of the livestock industry, where a few multinational corporations control a vast majority of the livestock".

Gibbons explains: "They are vertically integrated, from animal genetics to grocery store. What they charge isn't based upon what it costs to produce, and it's not based on supply and demand, because they know what they need to make a profit. What they have done, through government support and taxpayer support, is to intentionally overproduce so that the price stays low, sometimes below the cost of production. That kicks their competition out of the market. Then they become the only player in town.

"Over time, it has extracted wealth and power from communities. We can see how that has impacted rural main streets. You can see the boarded-up storefronts. You can see the lack of economic opportunity."

Gibbons says that corporations game the system by obtaining low-interest, federally guaranteed loans to build Cafos that then overproduce. But they know the government will buy up the surplus to stabilise prices.

"The system has been set up for the benefit of the factory farm corporations and their shareholders at the expense of family farmers, the real people, our environment, our food system," he adds.

"The thing that is really pervasive about it is that they control the rules of the game because they control the democratic process. It's a blueprint. We're paying for our own demise.

"It would be a different argument if it was just based upon inevitability or based on competition. But it's not based upon competition: it's based upon squelching competition."

There are about 70 million pigs in the US at any time, most of them destined for the dinner plate. But one in 10 are breeding sows, and the majority of those are in Cafos. The biggest pig farmer in the country is Virginia-based Smithfield Foods, which has nearly a million sows in the US (and more in Mexico and eastern Europe). Iowa Select Farms has one of the fastest-growing Cafo operations in the country, with 800 farms spread through half of the counties in Iowa.

Yet few of the economic benefits spill down to the communities around them. Workers are often poorly paid; many are bussed in. That they often include immigrants has sharpened the criticism from men like Nick Schutt, who used to work at Iowa Select, driving pigs in livestock trucks and handling sows. He says he earned $23,000 a year for 12-hour days and no overtime.

"These companies claim they're creating all these jobs, but who's coming? Not people with families who create communities."

Schutt lives in Williams, a small town in central Iowa, which is surrounded by Cafos and currently fighting to keep a big new one out, saying factory farms pollute the environment and depress property values. When the wind blows in the wrong direction, the stench from huge lakes of pig manure wafts across the town.

The high school Nick Schutt attended has closed. His daughter was in the last class to graduate. As Williams declined, the only doctor shut his clinic and left town. Schutt's mother used to own a restaurant: that closed along with the town's three grocery stores.

In Blairsburg, seven miles away, pretty much every shop except the post office is gone. The neighbouring hamlet of Wilke now consists of three animal sheds on land where dwellings were bulldozed from existence. Two-thirds of the counties in Iowa, almost all of them rural, have seen their populations decline since 2010, according to the US census.

North of Williams is a Cafo whose name, Quality Egg, has come to represent the worst of factory farming. In 1988, New York temporarily banned the sale of its eggs after salmonella killed 11 people. In 2017, its former owner, Jack DeCoster, went to prison, along with his son Peter, over a 2010 salmonella outbreak that made tens of thousands sick, left some with permanent injuries and prompted the recall of more than half a billion eggs shipped from Iowa factory farms. Quality Egg pleaded guilty to selling eggs with false expiry dates and to bribing an agriculture department inspector to approve the sale.

DeCoster had a long history of paying fines worth millions of dollars for animal cruelty, falsifying records, swindling contractors and polluting—without much impact on the way he did business. He was found to have made immigrant workers, many of them in the US illegally, live and work in squalid and unsafe conditions.

The company paid $1.5m to settle allegations that supervisors at Iowa plants raped female workers.

DeCoster is an extreme case, but around Iowa he's seen as emblematic of how the industry uses its money and influence to impose its will, including changing planning and environmental regulations.

Much of this is the result of agricultural corporations pouring millions into lobbying state governments. But Gibbons says Washington also bears some responsibility. He accuses President Barack Obama's administration of failing to deliver on promised reforms that would have benefited smaller farmers. It is this, he says, that damaged Obama's standing among farmers and drove up their support for Donald Trump.

Barb Kalbach is not optimistic about the future. Her son will not be taking over the farm. She hopes the land will stay in the family for at least another generation, but expects it to be rented out and subsumed into some larger operation.

But Kalbach fears something bigger than the loss of her own farm. Farmers are ageing and their children either have little interest in working the land or cannot afford the sophisticated equipment needed to compete with corporations.

"Investors buy the land, and they have tractors and combines that you can run by computer," she said. "They'll hire somebody to sit in a little office somewhere and run that stuff off the computer and farm the land that way. Now what you've done is you have lost the innate knowledge of how to grow food and raise animals. You've lost a whole generation of it, probably two. Now we are going to rely on a few corporations to decide who is going to eat and who isn't. We're one generation away from that picture right now."

In Williams, Schutt says he's seeing a community of owners becoming workers: "It's going to be like Russia with serfs. If you want to work on a farm, you'll have to work for them. We'll give you a job, but you're going to be working on our terms. We control everything. Small farms can't survive."

Kalbach agrees. "I think they're done," she said.

Overregulation of GMOs Is Not Beneficial

Beat Späth

Beat Späth is a director of agricultural biotechnology for EuropaBio.

The European Association for Bio-Industries (EuropaBio) says the decision by 16 EU nations to opt out of GMO crop cultivation has taken away the right of farmers to choose.

How have biotechnology companies reacted to this decision of 16 EU countries and four other regions?

We deeply regret that some EU countries have decided to make use of the new "licence to ban" on the cultivation of safe and approved GMO crops on their territories. European farmers, many of whom may have been interested in using GM technology in these territories, have officially lost their freedom to choose.

How will this affect investment and innovation by biotechnology multinationals in the region?

The new EU legislation allowing for these bans is a stop sign for agricultural innovation and sends a negative signal to all innovative industries considering investing in Europe. Much of the research has already been driven out of Europe. One indicator is the number of GM field trials, which have fallen from 109 in 2009 to 10 in 2014. Most research that remains in Europe in this field is focused on products for farmers outside the EU. There is still some laudable public GM research going on in parts of Europe, but even public researchers and public institutions face protests and illegal destructions of their field trials and the cost of protecting the fields

"Failing to Support GM Crops Single Most Damaging Element for Growth," by Beat Späth, India Environment Portal, October 14, 2015, http://re.indiaenvironmentportal.org.in/opinion/failing-support-gm-crops-single-most-damaging-element-growth. Licensed under CC BY-SA 2.5 IN.

from such illegal acts of vandalism is extremely high. In 2014, radical activists invaded the European Food Safety Authority with smoke bombs. German Nobel Prize laureate Christiane Nüsslein-Volhard said in March 2015 that most of the plant biotech students in Germany will have to emigrate to find jobs.

What according to you will be the next course of action for biotechnology multinationals in the region?

Europe lags behind the rest of the world when it comes to GM crop cultivation, to the detriment of European farmers and consumers. Due to the de facto and illegal moratorium on approvals of GMOs for cultivation, the majority of GM crops for cultivation have been withdrawn by the applicant companies after more than 10 years of waiting in the dysfunctional system.

Whilst there is little GM cultivation in the EU, the EU is a major importer of GM commodities from other parts of the world: we pay with GM cotton bank notes and wear GM cotton clothes, and we heavily rely on GM commodities to feed our farm animals. Each year, the EU imports over 33 million tonnes of genetically modified soya beans, totalling more than 60 kg for each of its 500 million citizens per year. This would tend to indicate that GM commodities have had and continue to have an important place in European agriculture.

Had your association expected a reaction of this scale in the region?

The biotechnology industry has been firmly and publicly opposed to the idea of opt-out clauses since the beginning because it is a very negative precedent of "politics over science" and represents one of the biggest investment disincentives for high-tech sectors. Moreover, it is very easy for some of the governments to ban GM cultivation where there are currently no GM crops suitable for their farmers. It will be interesting to see whether their choice will change when GM crops that would be adapted to their countries' needs become available and they find their farmers are at a competitive disadvantage to farmers that are able to access the technology in other parts of Europe or of the world.

Does the ban (as per the new EU law) apply only to GM maize which is MON810 GM? Are there any other varieties of GM maize or other GM crops affected by this ban?

Member States had the possibility to opt out from all authorisations granted and/or applications submitted before April 2, 2015. This includes the only GM crop currently cultivated in the EU—MON 810—and seven other GM products pending in the system for authorisation. The scoping-out demands of each Member State can be found here.

How do you think this will impact agricultural and biotechnology multinationals across the world planning to introduce GM crops? For example, the battle to promote genetically modified (GM) crops has gained momentum in South Asia and Southeast Asia. In Kenya, scientists are lobbying for approval to commercialise a genetically modified maize variety.

Biotech crops are the fastest adopted crop technology in the world. In 2014, global biotech crop hectarage continued to grow for the 19th consecutive year of commercialisation. According to International Service for the Acquisition of Agri-biotech Applications (ISAAA)'s figures, in 2014, 18 million farmers planted 181.5 million hectares of biotech crops in 28 countries, up from 175.2 million hectares in 27 countries in 2013. In other words there are more farmers cultivating GMOs in the world than there are farmers in all of Europe (circa 12 million), and GMOs grow on an area much larger than the EU's entire arable land (circa 104 million hectares). What is very important to note is that 90 per cent of these 18 million farmers were small resource-poor farmers, and for the third consecutive year, developing countries planted more biotech crops than industrial countries. More and more farmers planting more and more GM crops worldwide each year is a clear indication that this technology works and that, where allowed, farmers choose to grow GM crops.

Any other comment that you would like to share with us?

EuropaBio firmly believes that failing to support the EU's own best science is the single most damaging element for growth, innovation, investment as well as consumer confidence and safety. By banning the cultivation of safety-assessed GM crops, the Member States are officially denying their farmers the right to choose. Trillions of GM meals have been eaten over 19 years and in 2014, 18 million farmers planted biotech crops on 13 per cent of the world's arable land. Meanwhile, half of Europe chooses to turn the continent into a museum of agriculture without even asking its farmers.

The Green Revolution Didn't Deliver on Its Promise

Divya Sharma

Divya Sharma is a research fellow in agrarian transformations at the Science Policy Research Unit.

The dramatic increase in yields of wheat and rice in the 1960s and 1970s in India, along with many other countries in the post-colonial world, was framed as a technological breakthrough made possible by miracle hybrid seed varieties. This breakthrough ostensibly averted mass scale hunger and was central, so the story goes, to realising substantive national sovereignty in newly independent India.

We now know, after decades of extensive research, that yield increases were not all that dramatic. Expansion of monocultures, extensive use of agrochemicals, groundwater extraction, pricing and procurement policies were all just as critical, if not more so, than hybrid seed varieties for enhancing yield productivity.

Recent revisionist histories have further upended the simplified technological revolutionary narrative. They show how Cold War geopolitics engineered a systemic but deeply contested shift toward energy- and water-intensive agriculture. The so-called Green Revolution (GR) can be seen as another moment of incorporation of new sites in the long-standing and ongoing expansion of the industrial food system, albeit in the name of the small farmer and alleviating hunger.

My encounter with the GR has been through life stories of farmers in two regions, Punjab and Tamil Nadu, which have been the epicentres of agricultural intensification since the 1960s. Here, the social and material landscape has been transformed in distinctive ways, and the changes have been unevenly felt by

"What Is Revolutionary About the Green Revolution?" by Divya Sharma, STEPS Centre, June 17, 2019. Reprinted by permission.

farmers and workers in these spaces. In the south-west cotton belt of Punjab, where I have interacted with farmers and agroecology activists since 2012 for doctoral research, pests and pesticides dominate everyday conversations. Chemical contamination of water and soils, deteriorating health, rising incidence of particular diseases (e.g. cancer), reproductive health issues, and persistent crop damage due to pest attacks are in the foreground.

In Northern Tamil Nadu, where I have been working since 2017 as part of the Relational Pathways: Mapping Agency and Poverty Dynamics through Green Revolutions project, people's minds are occupied by drying open wells, erratic rainfall and frequent drought in recent years. The practice of cultivating rice three times a year, inaugurated with the GR, has come to a halt for most farmers, resulting in less work for women workers.

The stories of farmers and workers in these two regions suggest four big questions for Green Revolution thinking at this current political conjuncture in India.

What Drives the Calls for an Evergreen/ Second Green Revolution?

In recent years scientists and politicians have emphasised the need for transitioning toward sustainable agriculture, often obliquely acknowledging the failures of the current model. These calls for an "Evergreen" and "Second Green Revolution" refer to technologies, for example drip irrigation, soil cards for judicious use of agrochemicals, biotechnology, digital platforms for market and knowledge access, as well as new regional locations (Eastern India) and high-value crops (moving from wheat and rice to vegetables and fruits for instance).

While arguing for sustainability through the adoption of a novel approach, they are replete with old logics—including a Malthusian discourse to justify the need to close productivity gaps in new regions. They invoke the same extractive logic that defined the Green Revolution—the strategy of "betting on the strong"—which now means untapped water reservoirs, healthy soils and biodiverse landscapes. But what happens to the degraded, contaminated and water depleted landscapes of Punjab and Tamil Nadu, the granaries of the nation, as the Revolution moves east? Will the production of organic high-value crops cater to niche export markets and elite domestic consumers, or be geared toward addressing the challenge of widespread malnutrition and raising farm incomes?

How Is the Green Revolution Invoked in Narratives of Agrarian Crisis?

The pervasive narrative of agrarian crisis in India is centred on chronic indebtedness among cultivators and the unprofitability of farming. However, going beyond an economistic diagnosis that attributes the current distress to neoliberal reforms since the early the 1990s, A.R. Vasavi and others have stressed the need for a broader canvas for understanding the making of the rural socioecological crisis. This requires looking at the GR as part of the postcolonial development project, and the crisis as the failure of the promises it made. Jobless growth in the non-farm economy, coupled with the farming crisis, has thwarted rural people's aspirations for mobility—even as rural areas are becoming sites for further expansion of a consumer market. The systemic unevenness is underscored by the presence of farmers' suicides in regions of capital-intensive agriculture, not those excluded from agricultural modernisation.

How Do Resistance Narratives of Contemporary Agroecology Activism and Farmers' Movements Help Us Rethink the Green Revolution?

Narratives of the agrarian crisis have politicised the GR model of farming in the mainstream public discourse. Agroecology activists (such as the growing Zero Budget Natural Farming movement) and farmers' movements in different parts of the country are not only developing and mobilising alternative farming and food practices, but have also constructed an alternative narrative of the GR. They are bringing long-standing critiques of the GR from the fringes to the centre of the political discourse. These critiques challenge not just the impacts of the GR, but the fundamental underpinning assumptions about sovereignty, socio-ecological relations, knowledge production and development.

It is not only historians who are situating the GR within Cold War politics. In their village meetings, agroecology activists from Kheti Virasat Mission in Punjab discuss the repurposing of Second World War ammunition factories for fertiliser production, fertiliser that was dumped on farmers in newly decolonised countries. The large-scale co-ordinated protests by various farmers' and rural workers' groups in the last two years reinforces the multidimensional but connected experience of rural crisis.

How Do Cultivators and Workers Who Have Lived Through the GR Think of It Now?

Panchali, in her 70s now, has transplanted rice in other farmers' fields for most of her life in a GR village in Northern Tamil Nadu that has also been extensively researched since the 1970s. She does not recognise the term "Green Revolution" at all, but on further probing recalls the IR8 rice variety which did not last for long.

She also remembers a song about IR8 that women used to sing while transplanting. The lyrics talk about how IR8 rice brought debt to farm households, a male farmer drinking poison, and his wife and children are wondering what they are supposed to do after his death. The song could just as well be a rendering of the present agrarian crisis.

Her neighbour Sasidaran, who owns 16 acres and is a retired government school teacher, is known to be a technologically savvy "progressive farmer." Sasidaran procured hybrid rice varieties from the Philippines even before they were locally available through his contacts in the public extension system. According to him, the semi-arid North Arcot region had almost transformed into the Kaveri river delta in southern Tamil Nadu after the GR, but now he says, "it is turning into a desert, like your native place Rajasthan." The water level in the well on his land is erratic depending on rainfall, and he is gradually shifting to tree plantations instead of cultivating rice.

As rice cultivation becomes less frequent, older men and women workers dependent on transplanting sit on Panchali's porch during hot afternoons on most days to pass time and incant 'no rain, no work'. Another song that Panchali frequently sings for us on these afternoons is a lament to the rain gods, traditionally sung by widows, during an annual temple ritual in the summer months or during periods of drought.

For both Panchali and Sasidaran, the promise of postcolonial development encased in the GR narrative has been sucked out and displaced on to the many private educational institutions that are taking over agricultural lands along arterial roads and digging deep borewells. Farmers in this village attribute the drying of wells on their farms partly to the proliferation of these borewells that accompany real estate development.

After decades of studies on the GR in India, it is perhaps a truism to say that the diverse practices, experiences and adaptations by farmers and workers challenge any singular, linear GR narrative. But if their experiences could be distilled into a counter-narrative, it would perhaps be this: *IR8 and the deluge of rice varieties and agrochemicals will come and go, but the water is running out.* And rural people here are not investing their hopes in drip irrigation and soil cards either.

CHAPTER 4

Are Agricultural Practices Environmentally Sustainable?

Sustainable Agriculture Explained

Rinkesh Kukreja

Rinkesh Kukreja is the founder of the website Conserve Energy Future, *which is focused on energy conservation issues.*

The word sustainable has become very popular in recent years and it is now used to describe a lot of things. But what is sustainable agriculture? Simply put, sustainable agriculture is the production of plant and animal products, including food, in a way which uses farming techniques that protect the environment, public health, communities, and the welfare of animals. Sustainable agriculture allows us to produce and enjoy healthy foods without compromising the ability of future generations to do the same. The key to sustainable agriculture is finding the right balance between the need for food production and the preservation of environmental ecosystems. Sustainable agriculture also promotes economic stability for farms and helps farmers to better their quality of life. Agriculture continues to be the biggest employer in the world with 40% of the world's population working in it.

According to Wikipedia,

> Sustainable agriculture is the act of farming using principles of ecology, the study of relationships between organisms and their environment. It has been defined as "an integrated system of plant and animal production practices having a site-specific application that will last over the long term.

If given the choice I'm sure we would all choose to consume natural chemical free food instead of food that is sprayed with pesticides and chemical fertilizers. Sustainable agriculture differs greatly from industrial agriculture where large volumes of crops as well as livestock are produced for sale using industrial techniques. Industrial agriculture relies heavily on pesticides and chemical

"What is Sustainable Agriculture?" by Rinkesh Kukreja, Conserve Energy Future. Reprinted by permission.

fertilizers and other chemical enhancers. In the past decade the majority of food we ate has been grown in this manner. In 1996 only 20% of the corn in the United States was genetically modified, that number had reached 88% by 2006. However in the last couple of years, due to the negative aspects of the technique, there has been a slight shift towards the use of sustainable agricultural methods.

Methods of Sustainable Agriculture

1. **Crop Rotation:** Crop rotation is one of the most powerful techniques of sustainable agriculture. Its purpose is to avoid the consequences that come with planting the same crops in the same soil for years in a row. It helps tackle pest problems, as many pests prefer specific crops. If the pests have a steady food supply they can greatly increase their population size. Rotation breaks the reproduction cycles of pests. During rotation, farmers can plant certain crops, which replenish plant nutrients. These crops reduce the need for chemical fertilizers.

2. **Cover Crops:** Many farmers choose to have crops planted in a field at all times and never leave it barren, this can cause unintended consequences. By planting cover crops, such as clover or oats, the farmer can achieve his goals of preventing soil erosion, suppressing the growth of weeds, and enhancing the quality of the soil. The use of cover crops also reduces the need for chemicals such as fertilizers.

3. **Soil Enrichment:** Soil is a central component of agricultural ecosystems. Healthy soil is full of life, which can often be killed by the overuse of pesticides. Good soils can increase yields as well as creating more robust crops. It is possible to maintain and enhance the quality of soil in many ways. Some examples include leaving crop residue in the field after a harvest, and the use of composted plant material or animal manure.

4. **Natural Pest Predators:** In order to maintain effective control over pests, it is important to view the farm as an ecosystem as opposed to a factory. For example, many birds and other animals are in fact natural predators of agricultural pests. Managing your farm so that it can harbor populations of these pest predators is an effective as well as a sophisticated technique. The use of chemical pesticides can result in the indiscriminate killing of pest predators.

5. **Bio intensive Integrated Pest Management:** Integrated pest management (IPM). This is an approach, which really relies on biological as opposed to chemical methods. IMP also emphasizes the importance of crop rotation to combat pest management. Once a pest problem is identified, IPM will mean that chemical solutions will only be used as a last resort. Instead the appropriate responses would be the use of sterile males, and biocontrol agents such as ladybirds.

Benefits of Sustainable Agriculture

1. **Contributes to Environmental Conservation:** The environment plays a huge role in fulfilling our basic needs to sustain life. In turn, it is our duty to look after the environment so that future generations are not deprived of their needs. Sustainable agriculture helps to replenish the land as well as other natural resources such as water and air. This replenishment ensures that these natural resources will be able for future generations to sustain life.

2. **Public Health Safety:** Sustainable agriculture avoids hazardous pesticides and fertilizers. As a result, farmers are able to produce fruits, vegetables and other crops that are safer for consumers, workers, and surrounding communities. Through careful and proper management

of livestock waste, sustainable farmers are able to protect humans from exposure to pathogens, toxins, and other hazardous pollutants.

3. **Prevents Pollution:** Sustainable agriculture means that any waste a farm produces remains inside the farms ecosystem. In this way the waste cannot cause pollution.

4. **Reduction in Cost:** The use of sustainable agriculture reduces the need for fossil fuels, resulting in significant cost savings in terms of purchasing as well as transporting them. This in turn lessens the overall costs involved in farming.

5. **Biodiversity:** Sustainable farms produces a wide variety of plants and animals resulting in biodiversity. During crop rotation, plants are seasonally rotated and this results in soil enrichment, prevention of diseases, and pest outbreaks.

6. **Beneficial to Animals:** Sustainable agriculture results in animals being better cared for, as well as treated humanely and with respect. The natural behaviors of all living animals, including grazing or pecking, are catered for. As a result they develop in a natural way. Sustainable farmers and ranchers implement livestock husbandry practices that protect animals' health.

7. **Economically Beneficial For Farmers:** In exchange for engaging with sustainable farming methods, farmers receive a fair wage for their produce. This greatly reduces their reliance on government subsidies and strengthens rural communities. Organic farms typically require 2 ½ times less labor than factory farms yet yield 10 times the profit.

8. **Social Equality:** Practicing sustainable agriculture techniques also benefits workers as they are offered a more competitive salary as well as benefits. They also work in humane and fair working conditions, which

include a safe work environment, food, and adequate living conditions.

9. **Beneficial For Environment:** Sustainable agriculture reduces the need for use of non-renewable energy resources and as a result benefits the environment.

Due to population increase, it is estimated that by 2050 we will need approximately 70% more food than is currently being produced in order to provide the estimated 9.6 billion world population with their recommended daily calorie intake. This is by no means a small challenge, but unlike many other sustainability challenges, everyone can play a part. We all need to eat, but by simply reducing food loss and waste, as well as eating diets that are lower impact, and investing in sustainable produce, we can make a difference. From countries, to companies, right down to consumers, we all have a role to play. The challenge is simply making people care in a world where we are surrounded by such abundance.

Agroecology Can Be a Positive Force for the Future of Farming

The Committee on World Food Security

The Committee on World Food Security is a body of the United Nations that is dedicated to food security and nutrition for all.

Addressing the challenges facing our global food system—from rising demand to rising temperatures—requires concerted action from across the agricultural sector and its value chain.

Agroecology has returned to the global spotlight, as one approach to bring farmers closer to meeting these challenges. Agroecology emerged as a science which supports food security and sustainable agriculture. In the 1960s, it was studied as the interaction between crops and the environment. In short, it can help us understand agriculture's impact on our natural resource base.

Since then, many definitions of agroecology have evolved. Promoting farming systems that are beneficial to producers and society, as well as the earth's ecosystems has become a central theme, prompting the concept of agroecology to become synonymous with outcomes such as resource use efficiency, optimizing external inputs and improving soil health.

Here are six ways this can be done, as featured in Farming First's "Agroecology in Action" blog series.

Harnessing the Potential of Orphan Crops

While the world gets the majority of its calories from just three staple crops, the many neglected varieties that are grown regionally offer huge potential for improving food and nutrition security, particularly in Africa. These crops are often already adapted to regional conditions but are "orphan" because they have not

"Six Ways Agroecology Can Help Shape the Future of Farming," Farming First, The Committee on World Food Security, October 26, 2018. Reprinted by permission.

received the same level of attention from scientists to improve or optimise them.

The African Orphan Crops Consortium (AOCC) is working to preserve and improve these species so they can continue to perform important functions within a diverse ecosystem while nourishing people.

Maximising Natural Processes

Agriculture requires a regular harvesting of crops. This results in large amounts of vital nutrients being removed from the soil. We must return these vital components to the soil, to ensure its health and sustainability.

With the help of rhizobium bacteria, soybean can naturally fix nitrogen from the air into the soil, which helps support optimum soil health and plant growth. For major soybean producers like Brazil, making best use of this natural ability to replenish soil minimises environmental impact while maximising productivity. However, soybeans cannot grow with nitrogen alone; they also need phosphorus. As there is no natural process to fix phosphorus into the soil, it must be added in the form of mineral fertilizers, applied carefully in the correct amounts. Natural and manmade innovations can work together in this way to achieve important agroecological outcomes, such as improved soil health.

Keeping Pests at Bay In the Safest Way

There is no single failsafe solution for crop pests like Fall Armyworm: farmers need to make use of all available tools and solutions. The first port of call is a biological approach, which can range from simple sticky traps to sophisticated microbial inoculants, which are referred to as "beneficial bacteria" that are developed from a crop's natural enemies, such as bacteria, fungi and viruses. If this proves insufficient, farmers need to be equipped with the knowledge to use crop protection products safely and efficiently.

In Honduras, Fintrac has trained farmers on how to triple wash and perforate pesticide containers, which were then collected by safe disposal service teams. One of those farmer clients, Emiliano Dominiquez, who had been in danger of having his food and income source wiped out by aphids, instead saw crop yields increase six-fold as a result of integrating integrated pest management into his on-farm practices.

Encouraging Forest-Friendly Farming

In Ethiopia, Farm Africa have been working with farmers to develop forest-friendly businesses such as bee-keeping and forest coffee production, which incentivise farmer-reforestation efforts. In the Bale region alone, the combination of income from forest enterprises and the anticipation of income from the sale of carbon credits has saved 12,496 hectares of forest between 2012 and 2015. This is one way the needs of rural people to utilize natural resources to eat and earn a living, can be balanced with the need to protect the environment.

Using Data and Technology to Improve Farmer Decision-Making

Smart handheld digital devices that can be deployed for scientific measuring and testing to enhance production and marketing are taking off. Pocket-sized sensors that detect the amount of nitrogen a plant requires, for example are now being used on African farms. The data collected helps farmers make better decisions on precisely how much fertilizer to apply, to reduce loss into the environment. Known as "precision agriculture," this high-tech approach will go a long way to helping farmers put good agricultural practices into action, and move closer to farming systems that improve the health of the overall agroecosystem.

Optimizing External Inputs

Optimizing external inputs and improving soil health are two key agrocological outcomes the United Nations has identified. Work to achieve this in sub-Saharan Africa, where inputs are less accessible and soil health is poor, is well underway.

The African Agricultural Technology Foundation is applying biotechnology approaches to produce rice that is both efficient in its use of nitrogen and water. This means the 20 million or more smallholder farmers that depend on rice as a staple food need to use less of these two crucial inputs. Less nitrogen is lost, soils become healthier, and crops can grow even when water is scarce.

Regenerative Agriculture Promotes Environmentally Sustainable Agricultural Methods

Stephanie Anderson

Stephanie Anderson is a journalist and writer of narrative nonfiction and literary fiction. Anderson is the author of One Size Fits None: A Farm Girl's Search for the Promise of Regenerative Agriculture *(2019).*

For years, "sustainable" has been the buzzword in conversations about agriculture. If farmers and ranchers could slow or stop further damage to land and water, the thinking went, that was good enough. I thought that way too, until I started writing my new book, "One Size Fits None: A Farm Girl's Search for the Promise of Regenerative Agriculture."

I grew up on a cattle ranch in western South Dakota and once worked as an agricultural journalist. For me, agriculture is more than a topic—it is who I am. When I began working on my book, I thought I would be writing about sustainability as a response to the environmental damage caused by conventional agriculture—farming that is industrial and heavily reliant on oil and agrochemicals, such as pesticides and fertilizers.

But through research and interviews with farmers and ranchers around the United States, I discovered that sustainability's "give back what you take" approach, which usually just maintains or marginally improves resources already degraded by generations of conventional agriculture, does not adequately address the biggest long-term challenge farmers face: climate change.

But there is an alternative. A method called regenerative agriculture promises to create new resources, restoring them to preindustrial levels or better. This is good for farmers as well as the environment, since it lets them reduce their use of agrochemicals while making their land more productive.

What Holds Conventional Farmers Back

Modern American food production remains predominantly conventional. Growing up in a rural community of farmers and ranchers, I saw firsthand why.

As food markets globalized in the early 1900s, farmers began specializing in select commodity crops and animals to increase profits. But specialization made farms less resilient: If a key crop failed or prices tumbled, they had no other income source. Most farmers stopped growing their own food, which made them dependent on agribusiness retailers.

Under these conditions small farms consolidated into large ones as families went bankrupt—a trend that continues today. At the same time, agribusiness companies began marketing new machines and agrochemicals. Farmers embraced these tools, seeking to stay in business, specialize further and increase production.

In the 1970s, the government's position became "Get big or get out" under Earl Butz, who served as Secretary of Agriculture from 1971 to 1976. In the years since, critics like the nonprofit Food and Water Watch have raised concerns that corporate representatives have dictated land grant university research by obtaining leadership positions, funding agribusiness-friendly studies, and silencing scientists whose results conflict with industrial principles.

These companies have also shaped government policies in their favor, as economist Robert Albritton describes in his book "Let Them Eat Junk." These actions encouraged the growth of large industrialized farms that rely on genetically modified seeds, agrochemicals and fossil fuel.

Several generations into this system, many conventional farmers feel trapped. They lack the knowledge required to farm without inputs, their farms are big and highly specialized, and most are carrying operating loans and other debts.

In contrast, regenerative agriculture releases farmers from dependence on agribusiness products. For example, instead of purchasing synthetic fertilizers for soil fertility, producers rely on diverse crop rotations, no-till planting and management of livestock grazing impacts.

Agribusiness dogma says that regenerative agriculture cannot feed the world and or ensure a healthy bottom line for farmers, even as conventional farmers are going bankrupt. I have heard this view from people I grew up with in South Dakota and interviewed as a farm journalist.

"Everybody seems to want smaller local producers," Ryan Roth, a farmer from Belle Glade, Florida told me. "But they can't keep up. It's unfortunate. I think it's not the best development for agriculture operations to get bigger, but it is what we're dealing with."

The Climate Threat

Climate change is making it increasingly hard for farmers to keep thinking this way. The United Nations Intergovernmental Panel on Climate Change (IPCC) has warned that without rapid action to reduce greenhouse gas emissions over roughly the next decade, warming will trigger devastating impacts such as wildfires, droughts, floods and food shortages.

For farmers, large-scale climate change will cause decreased crop yields and quality, heat stress for livestock, disease and pest outbreaks, desertification on rangelands, changes in water availability and soil erosion.

As I explain in my book, regenerative agriculture is an effective response to climate change because producers do not use agrochemicals—many of which are derived from fossil fuels—and greatly reduce their reliance on oil. The experiences of farmers who have adopted regenerative agriculture show that it restores soil carbon, literally locking carbon up underground, while also reversing desertification, recharging water systems, increasing biodiversity and reducing greenhouse gas emissions. And it produces nutrient-rich food and promises to enliven rural communities and reduce corporate control of the food system.

No Single Model

How farmers put this strategy into practice differs depending on their location, goals and community needs. Regenerative agriculture is a one-size-fits-none model of farming that allows for flexibility and close tailoring to individual environments.

At Great Plains Buffalo in South Dakota, for example, rancher Phil Jerde is reversing desertification on the grassland. Phil moves buffalo across the land in a way that mimics their historic movement over the Great Plains, rotating them frequently through small pastures so they stay bunched together and impact the land evenly via their trampling and waste distribution. The land has adequate time to rest and regrow between rotations.

After transitioning his conventional ranch to a regenerative one over 10 years, Phil saw bare ground revert back to prairie grassland. Water infiltration into the ground increased, his herd's health improved, wildlife and insect populations recovered and native grasses reappeared.

On Brown's Ranch in North Dakota, farmer Gabe Brown also converted his conventional operation to a regenerative one in a decade. He used a combination of cover crops, multicropping (growing two or more crops on a piece of land in a single season), intercropping (growing two or more crops together), an intensive rotational grazing system called mob grazing, and no-till farming to restore soil organic matter levels to just over 6 percent—roughly the level most native prairie soils contained before settlers plowed them up. Restoring organic matter sequesters carbon in the soil, helping to slow climate change.

Conventional farmers often worry about losing the illusion of control that agrochemicals, monocultures and genetically modified seeds provide. I asked Gabe how he overcame these fears. He replied that one of the most important lessons was learning to embrace the environment instead of fighting it.

"Regenerative agriculture can be done anywhere because the principles are the same," he said. "I always hear, 'We don't get the moisture or this or that.' The principles are the same everywhere. There's nature everywhere. You're just mimicking nature is all you're doing."

The Future

Researchers with Project Drawdown, a nonprofit that spotlights substantive responses to climate change, estimate that land devoted to regenerative agriculture worldwide will increase from 108 million acres currently to 1 billion acres by 2050. More resources are appearing to help farmers make the transition, such as investment groups, university programs and farmer-to-farmer training networks.

Organic food sales continue to rise, suggesting that consumers want responsibly grown food. Even big food companies like General Mills are embracing regenerative agriculture.

The question now is whether more of America's farmers and ranchers will do the same.

Organic Agriculture Is Sustainable Agriculture

Mary Wales

Mary Wales is a writer and communications and marketing professional who focuses on healthy and sustainable food and agriculture. She is based in Toronto, Canada.

Sustainability and the environment are top of mind for many today. Issues like smog, rising global temperatures, water pollution, and oodles of plastic waste have many concerned. Many people also question how their food is grown whether through conventional or organic means—and if it's grown sustainably or not. Organic food offers a more sustainable, long term solution for 4 main reasons:

1. Organic farming rebuilds soil health and stops harmful chemicals from getting into our water supplies. Water and soil are two *extremely* important resources necessary for growing food.
2. Organic farmers don't rely on non-renewable oil-based fertilizers and pesticides we may not always have access to.
3. Organic farming results in greater biodiversity.
4. Organic farming releases fewer greenhouse gas emissions.

Reason #1: Less Soil and Water Pollution

Soil and water pollution are two major problems today, and non-organic food production is surely a big part of this problem. According to the Food and Agriculture Organization of the United Nations (UN FAO), about 1/3 or the world's soil has already been degraded because of "chemical heavy" farming techniques, and deforestation, which increases erosion and global warming.

"Why Organic Food Is More Sustainable," by Mary Wales, Nature's Path Foods, May 1, 2018. Reprinted by permission.

- Soil is such an important resource for growing food, and the UN FAO reports that to generate just 3 centimetres of top soil takes 1000 years!
- Our water, another extremely valuable farming resource, is also at risk. In a long-term study by the United States Geological Society, pesticide compounds were found in streams almost 100% of the time.

Organically grown and produced food does not use the typical agri-chemical fertilizers and pesticides that can deplete soils over time and pollute our water supplies. Organic farmers follow strict regulations and work to rebuild soil health naturally.

Reason #2: Oil-Based Fertilizers and Pesticides

For many people, whether or not something is sustainable depends on whether it could last for generations to come. Many agree oil isn't something that's going to last for generations to come, and the world will eventually face an end of the "oil era". As the world moves away from oil, gas and coal and towards more renewable forms of energy, like wind and solar, many people are also looking food grown without the use of oil-based fertilizers and pesticides. Under organic production, synthetic, oil-based pesticides and fertilizers are not allowed. Rather, organic farmers produce food with natural fertilisers and less energy, and they must follow strict rules about what inputs can be used.

Reason #3: Greater Biodiversity

It's no secret that our wildlife is under threat because of chemical agricultural practices. A recent study found that birds in France, for example, have declined by a third in the past 15 years because of changes in agricultural practices, including pesticide use. Another study published last year also found that vast numbers of insects—including helpful pollinators like bees—are dying off.

Organic farming is beneficial for wildlife: According to scholar John Reganold of Washington State University, organic agriculture results in greater biodiversity of plants, animals, insects and microbes. An analysis of 66 scientific studies showed that organic farms have 30% more species on average than non-organic ones.

Reason #4: Fewer Greenhouse Gas Emissions

Climate change is a serious global threat—with agriculture and food production being major contributors to this threat and the release of greenhouse gases. Although estimates vary, the Consultative Group on International Agricultural Research reports that 1/3 of our greenhouse gas emissions come from agriculture and food production, which agricultural production and growing food accounting for the "lion's share" of emissions. The UN FAO reports that unless we make an effort to reduce these greenhouse gas emissions, they could increase greatly in the near future.

Studies like this one here have found that organic farms release a lot less greenhouse gas emissions than non-organic farms. Healthy soils are a major source of carbon storage, and organic farming results in increased carbon sequestration. The U.K.'s Soil Association estimates that if all U.K. farming was converted to organic, at least 1.3 million tonnes of carbon would be taken up by the soil each year. That's the equivalent of taking nearly 1 million cars off the road!

The Choice Is Clear

Eating organic is eating sustainably! Organic food is a long-term solution resulting in less soil and water pollution, a decreased reliance on oil-based fertilizers and pesticides, greater biodiversity, and less greenhouse gas emissions.

Agriculture Has Been a Source of Water Pollution, but New Efforts Are Being Made to Reverse Course

Food and Agriculture Organization of the United Nations

The Food and Agriculture Organization of the United Nations (FAO) is a specialized agency of the United Nations that leads international efforts to defeat hunger.

Agriculture, which accounts for 70 percent of water withdrawals worldwide, plays a major role in water pollution. Farms discharge large quantities of agrochemicals, organic matter, drug residues, sediments and saline drainage into water bodies.

Diagnosis, prediction and monitoring are key requirements for the management of agricultural practices that mitigate these harmful impacts on water resources, according to a new publication released today. The executive summary of Water Pollution from Agriculture: A Global Review, A Global Review, a precursor to the launch of the full report next year, highlights that water pollution is an increasing global concern that damages economic growth and the health of billions of people.

According to the report—from the Food and Agriculture Organization of the United Nations (FAO) and the Water, Land and Ecosystems (WLE) program led by the International Water Management Institute —exploding demand for food with high environmental footprints, such as meat from industrial farms, is contributing to unsustainable agricultural intensification and to water-quality degradation.

This growth in crop production has been achieved mainly through the intensive use of inputs such as pesticides and chemical fertilizers. Today, the global market in pesticides is worth more than USD 35 billion per year. Some countries—such as Argentina, Malaysia, South Africa and Pakistan—have experienced double-digit growth in the intensity of pesticide use.

"In most high-income countries and many emerging economies, agricultural pollution has overtaken contamination from settlements and industries as the main factor in the degradation of inland and coastal waters," said Eduardo Mansur, Director of FAO's Land and Water Division. "Acknowledging we have a problem is the first step to finding solutions."

The area equipped for irrigation has more than doubled in recent decades, from 139 million hectares in 1961 to 320 million in 2012, transferring agricultural pollution to water bodies.

Meanwhile, the total number of livestock has risen from 7.3 billion units in 1970 to 24.2 billion units in 2011. Livestock production now accounts for 70 percent of all agricultural land and 30 percent of the planet's land surface.

Additionally, aquaculture has grown more than 20-fold since the 1980s, particularly in Asia. Total global aquatic animal production reached 167 million tonnes in 2014. Fish excreta and uneaten feeds from fed aquaculture diminish water quality. Increased production has combined with greater use of antibiotics, fungicides and anti-fouling agents, which may contribute to polluting downstream ecosystems.

Nitrate from agriculture is now the most common chemical contaminant in the world's groundwater aquifers. Aquatic ecosystems are affected by agricultural pollution; for example, eutrophication caused by the accumulation of nutrients in lakes and coastal waters impacts biodiversity and fisheries. Despite data gaps, 415 coastal areas have been identified experiencing eutrophication.

Meanwhile, about one-quarter of produced food is lost along the food-supply chain, accounting for 24 percent of the freshwater resources used in food-crop production, 23 percent of total global cropland area and 23 percent of total global fertilizer use.

As a result of all of the above, 38 percent of water bodies in the European Union are under pressure from agricultural pollution.

In the US, agriculture is the main source of pollution in rivers and streams, the second main source in wetlands and the third main source in lakes. In China, agriculture is responsible for a large share of surface-water pollution and is responsible almost exclusively for groundwater pollution by nitrogen.

This pollution poses demonstrated risks to aquatic ecosystems, human health and productive activities. For example, high levels of nitrates in water can cause "blue baby syndrome", a potentially fatal illness in infants.

In Organization for Economic Co-operation and Development (OECD) countries alone, the environmental and social costs of water pollution caused by agriculture are estimated to exceed billions of dollars annually.

And, over the last 20 years, a new class of agricultural pollutants has emerged in the form of veterinary medicines (antibiotics, vaccines and growth promoters), which move from farms through water to ecosystems and drinking water sources. But there are ways to deal with these issues, the report finds.

Policies and Initiatives

The right policies and incentives can encourage diets that are more sustainable and healthy and so moderate increases in food demand. For example, financial incentives such as taxes and subsidies on food and coupons for consumers positively influence dietary behavior. Food losses and waste should be reduced to minimize the waste of resources and associated environmental impacts.

A broader range of measures policy measures addressing other areas has also evolved. Recent analyses suggest that a combination of approaches (regulations, economic incentives and information) works better than regulations alone.

On-Farm Responses

On-farm practices in crop production, livestock and aquaculture are crucial for preventing pollution. In crop production, management measures for reducing the risk of water pollution due to organic and inorganic fertilizers and pesticides include limiting and optimizing the type, amount and timing of applications to crops.

Establishing protection zones along surface watercourses, within farms and in buffer zones around farms, have been shown to be effective in reducing pollution migration to water bodies.

Also, efficient irrigation schemes will reduce water return flows and therefore can greatly reduce the migration of fertilizers and pesticides to water bodies.

Off-Farm Responses

The best way of mitigating pressures on aquatic ecosystems is to avoid or limit the export of pollutants. Simple off-farm techniques, such as riparian buffer strips or constructed wetlands, can cost-effectively reduce loads entering surface water bodies.

Buffer strips are a well-established technology. Vegetated filter strips at the margins of farms and along rivers are effective in decreasing concentrations of pollutants entering waterways.

Integrated systems in which crops, vegetables, livestock, trees and fish are managed collectively can increase production stability, resource use efficiency and environmental sustainability. Integrated farming ensures that waste from one enterprise becomes inputs to another, thereby helping to optimize the use of resources and reduce pollution.

Before any action, to design cost-effective measures for preventing pollution and mitigating risks, managers, planners and lawmakers need to know the state of aquatic ecosystems, the nature and dynamics of the drivers and pressures that lead to water-quality degradation, and the impacts of such degradation on human health and the environment.

"This report lays out many ways to reduce pollution through tried-and-tested methods, as well as emerging options," said Mansur. "We now have to step up the pace of our efforts to meet the goal of the 2030 Agenda to provide a more-sustainable and fairer world for all."

Agriculture Is a Cause of Disappearing Biodiversity

Organic Without Boundaries

Organic Without Boundaries is a blog operated by IFOAM-Organics International, an umbrella organization for the organic agriculture movement.

FAO recently launched the first-ever global report on "The State of the World's Biodiversity for Food and Agriculture" presenting mounting and worrying evidence that the biodiversity sustaining our food systems is disappearing. This puts the future of our food, livelihoods, health, and environment under severe threat.

Once lost, the report warns all species that support our food systems and sustain the people who grow and/or provide our food cannot be recovered. On a positive note, biodiversity-friendly farming practices such as organic are helping to counter this scenario.

Biodiversity—The Variety of Life Found on Earth

Biodiversity for food and agriculture is all the plants and animals—wild and domesticated that provide food, feed, fuel, and fiber. It is also the myriad of organisms that support food production through ecosystem services, called "associated biodiversity." This includes all the plants, animals and micro-organisms such as insects, bats, birds, mangroves, corals, seagrasses, earthworms, soil-dwelling fungi and bacteria that keep soils fertile, pollinate plants, purify water and air, keep fish and trees healthy, and fight crop and livestock pests and diseases.

The report, prepared by the Food and Agricultural Organization of the United Nations (FAO) under the guidance of the Commission on Genetic Resources for Food and Agriculture looks at all these

"The Disappearance of Biodiversity Crucial for Food & Agriculture," Organic Without Boundaries, March 22, 2019. Reprinted by permission.

elements. It is based on information provided specifically by 91 countries, and the analysis of the latest global data.

Food Systems Under Severe Threat

Several key components of biodiversity for food and agriculture at genetic, species and ecosystem levels are in decline. The diversity of crops present in farmers' fields has declined and threats to crop diversity are increasing.

Many species, including pollinators, soil organisms and the natural enemies of pests, that contribute to vital ecosystem services are in decline as a consequence of the destruction and degradation of habitats, overexploitation, pollution, and other threats.

There is also a rapid decline in key ecosystems that deliver numerous services essential to food and agriculture, including the supply of freshwater, protection against storms, floods, and other hazards, and habitats for species such as fish and pollinators.

Leading Causes of Biodiversity Loss

The driver of biodiversity loss for food and agriculture cited by most reporting countries changes in land and water use and management. This is followed by pollution, overexploitation and overharvesting, climate change, as well as population growth and urbanization.

Demographic changes, urbanization, markets, trade, and consumer preferences strongly influence food systems, frequently with negative consequences on biodiversity and the ecosystem services it provides.

Such drivers can though also open opportunities to make food systems more sustainable, for example through the development of markets for biodiversity-friendly products such as organic food and beverages.

Biodiversity-Friendly Solutions

FAO's report also highlights a growing interest in biodiversity-friendly practices and approaches e.g. 80% of the 91 countries indicate using one or more biodiversity-friendly practice such as organic agriculture, integrated pest management, and agroecology.

This supports the findings unearthed by Solution Search: Farming for Biodiversity, a global competition run by Rare and IFOAM-Organics International in 2017.

Following the competition, the "Farming for Biodiversity" report was released showcasing 338 community-based solutions that help farmers and other agricultural practitioners adopt ecologically-friendly practices that protect biodiversity.

These innovations contribute to biodiversity protection in many ways by employing methods with an emphasis on agroecology, organic farming, integrated farming, and conservation agriculture to replace the overuse of chemical fertilizers and pesticides, and to restore ecosystems.

They take better control of waste and crop residues, including producing compost, animal feed, or biofuel. They bring new-found economic benefits and recognition for traditional varieties, knowledge, and practices and also celebrate the potential of youth and women farmers as drivers of change.

Time to Act, But How?

Biodiversity-focused practices are often complex and require a good understanding of local ecosystems. According to FAO several countries noted major challenges in up-scaling such practices, and there is a need to promote them through capacity development and the strengthening of policy frameworks.

Here, the "Farming for Biodiversity" report delivers assistance as it highlights the success factors solutions have in common, allowing for replication, as well as the design of global policy frameworks needed to stop rapid biodiversity loss.

Steps to Be Taken Include

- Transforming attitudes towards nature by boosting social awareness and behavior change;
- Tailoring initiatives to ecological and economic contexts;

- Identifying and strengthening local champions of biodiversity;
- Setting incentives and economic returns to create win/wins, and
- Creating spaces and support for bottom-up community engagement.

Supporting Policies

To identify policy frameworks that have proven successful on this and other aspects of sustainability, IFOAM—Organics International teamed up with FAO and the World Future Council to run a global contest for laws and policies that work best in supporting agroecology.

Future Outlook

Overall, there is a need to improve collaboration among policy-makers, producer organizations, consumers, the private sector and civil society organizations across food and agriculture and environment sectors.

Opportunities to develop more markets for biodiversity-friendly products could be explored and we can also look at the role citizens can play in reducing pressure on biodiversity e.g. by choosing sustainably/organically grown products or avoiding the purchase of foods considered unsustainable.

Surprisingly, Organic Farming Is Not Always Environmentally Safe or Friendly

Javier Yanes

Javier Yanes is a freelance editor and writer who has written for the Banco Bilbao Vizcaya Argentaria Group's OpenMind project.

In 1964, the biochemist and science fiction author Isaac Asimov predicted that at the beginning of the 21st century our nutrition would be based on precooked food, and that we would only reserve a small corner in our kitchens to prepare a dish when visitors came. He could not have been more wrong. Instead of the alienation of nature that Asimov predicted, the new century has brought the opposite trend, the return to the natural, with the consumption of organic food as one of its main banners. And although there is some controversy about whether these products are actually healthier or more nutritious than conventional ones, something that no one would deny is that they are more environmentally friendly. But are they?

Even in this case, reality seems to be more complex than appearances. Putting aside the differences due to the rules that each country can establish about what is considered an organically produced food, in general it would be said that the environmental impact of these products should be lower, due to the fact that synthetic pesticides (or *chemicals* in common language) are not used.

The keyword is "synthetic"; contrary to what a huge majority of consumers of these products understand, organic agriculture does in fact employ pesticides, although they must also be organic. But as some experts have warned, natural pesticides are not necessarily less toxic than synthetic pesticides. And since they often have to be used in larger quantities, their environmental impact may be

"Organic Farming: Not Always So Environmentally Friendly," by Javier Yanes, OpenMind, Banco Bilbao Vizcaria Argentaria Group, February 5, 2019. Reprinted by permission.

higher than conventional ones, as revealed in a 2010 study by the University of Guelph (Canada) that compared the use of synthetic and organic insecticides in the cultivation of soy.

Environmental Impact of Organic Farms

Soil pollution is not the only aspect in which organic production can fail to fulfil its promise of sustainability. In 2012, researchers from the University of Oxford (United Kingdom) analysed 71 previous studies to compare the environmental impact of organic farms and conventional farms. The results indicated that organic farms generally host 30% more biodiversity and their environmental footprint is less per unit of land, but conversely it is not always so per unit of product: while cattle and olive cultivation are more friendly with the environment in their organic versions, pigs, milk and cereals actually generate are more greenhouse gases per unit of product than their conventional equivalents.

According to the director of the study, Hanna Tuomisto, "whilst some organic farming practices do have less environmental impact than conventional ones, the published evidence suggests that others are actually worse for some aspects of the environment. The researcher points out that "people need to realise that an *organic* label is not a straightforward guarantee of the most environmentally-friendly product."

One of the factors that raise the environmental cost of organic product is that more land must be used to generate the same volume of food, due to the lower use of fertilizers. This need to devote greater acreage to agricultural production leads to deforestation that reduces the storage capacity of carbon in soils. The final effect is an increase in greenhouse gas emissions responsible for climate change.

This effect is evident in a study published last December in the journal *Nature*. The authors analysed two specific crops in Sweden, reaching the conclusion that organic peas have a 50% higher climate impact than conventional ones, while this difference increases to almost 70% in the case of wheat.

Soils with Less Carbon

The principal novelty of the study is that the authors have developed a standardised methodology to measure the opportunity cost of the land in terms of carbon storage. Previous research has compared the direct emissions of greenhouse gases in organic and conventional production, but according to the authors, the indirect effect due to the alternative uses of the land if it were not devoted to agriculture is often underestimated.

The authors point out that, thanks to international trade, this effect is transmitted from one region to another. "Agriculture always uses land," study director Timothy Searchinger of Princeton University (USA) tells *OpenMind*. "If there are lower yields on one hectare of land, then to produce the same food, you need to have more land producing food elsewhere, and that means this land is storing less carbon," says Searchinger. "If you are in a country that is not deforesting land, food production still has to come from somewhere."

In turn, this environmental cost of organic farming is transmitted to livestock. However, the authors clarify that each product is a particular case, and therefore the most ecologically responsible options consist of the choice of specific foods: "For example, eating organic beans or organic chicken is much better for the climate than eating conventionally produced beef," says study co-author Stefan Wirsenius, from Chalmers University of Technology (Sweden). In general, chicken, pork, fish, eggs or vegetables have a lower climate impact than cattle and sheep.

Biofuels, a Not-So-Green Alternative

A particularly surprising case is that of biofuels, used throughout the world as a green alternative to fossil fuels. According to the analysis of Searchinger, Wirsenius and his collaborators, this premise does not hold. From the point of view of its total impact on climate, after adding direct emissions and the opportunity cost of carbon, "it is better to use fossil fuels than biofuels," says Searchinger. This is due to the large tracts of land occupied by the crops from which the biofuels are extracted; it does not apply to those obtained from waste.

However, says Searchinger, this does not mean that fossil fuels are the best option, but rather that, "the same money that is now being put into biofuels in the name of climate change that actually increases greenhouse gas emissions could be put into other approaches to reduce emissions." And regarding which, Searchinger is clear about what is needed: "As rapid as possible a transition toward electric vehicles."

Animal Agriculture Is a Cause of Climate Change

ProVeg International

ProVeg is an international food awareness organization that aims to reduce the global consumption of animal products by 50 percent by the year 2040.

Climate change is a threat to food security, water availability, and biodiversity worldwide, as well as a major cause of environmental disasters. The production and consumption of animal products is a major driver of climate change, whereas adopting a plant-based diet helps to reduce greenhouse gas emissions. ProVeg raises awareness of the connection between our diets and climate change, and provides solutions that make dietary change easier than ever before.

What Is Climate Change?

Since the dawn of industrialisation, the average global temperature has been gradually increasing. A great deal of research has shown that this increase is due to human activities, and that climate change is rapidly transforming the world we live in. It is already affecting the environment, economy, and society in a variety of ways, and will increasingly influence our daily lives as well. While climate change is marked by long-term incremental changes such as slowly rising temperatures and sea levels, it will also result in a greater number of extreme weather events such as storms, floods, and exceptionally hot summers. These will impact negatively on agriculture, general productivity, and human health. Additionally, climate change results in increased incidences of heat waves that are especially dangerous for children and elderly people.

"The impact of animal agriculture on climate change," Proveg International, March 21, 2018. Reprinted by permission.

The Role of Animal Agriculture in Climate Change

Meat, dairy, and egg production are among the leading causes of human-caused climate change, soil erosion, water pollution, and the decrease in biodiversity. According to the FAO (Food and Agricultural Organization of the United Nations), farmed animals are responsible for 14.5% of total greenhouse gas emissions. Animal agriculture also accounts for at least half of all food-related greenhouse gas emissions.[1, 2] In total, the global food system contributes about 30% of all human-made emissions.[3, 4] Worldwide, the top 20 meat and dairy corporations produce more greenhouse gas emissions than the whole of Germany.[5]

Direct Emissions: Methane and Nitrous Oxide from Animal Husbandry

While carbon dioxide is the most notorious greenhouse gas, responsible for about 27% of animal agriculture's greenhouse gas emissions,[6] methane is potentially 28 times more harmful than carbon dioxide in terms of its global warming potential, while nitrous oxide is 265 times as potent.[7] The greatest source of the former is cattle, who, like all ruminants (cows, sheep and goats), produce methane during their digestive process. This gas is responsible for about 44% of animal agriculture's total greenhouse gas emissions.[8] Nitrous oxide, on the other hand, is released when animal manure is used as fertiliser, composted, or otherwise processed. It is especially problematic if more nitrogen is used than the vegetation can absorb. About 29% of the meat industry's emissions are in the form of nitrous oxide.[9] The immense scale of beef and dairy production means that cattle farming contributes the biggest share of the meat industry's total greenhouse gas emissions, at 65%.[10] Emission levels continue to rise due to ever-intensifying meat and dairy production.

Indirect Emissions: Land Use Changes Promote Climate Change

Besides being a huge source of emissions, animal agriculture further exacerbates climate change as vast areas of forests, grasslands, and wetlands are cleared to provide land for grazing and to grow animal feed crops. Forests and other wildlands mitigate climate change by acting as massive carbon sinks, in which carbon is absorbed from the atmosphere and sequestered underground.

Deforestation Has Serious Consequences for the Environment

Often referred to as "the lungs of the earth", the Amazon rainforest is critical to regulating the world's climate and weather cycles. Yet a staggering 20% has already been destroyed, and an equally big area is facing the same threat.[11] If the destruction of the Amazon rainforest continues unchecked, we will reach a point of no return, which could lead to the complete collapse of the Amazonian ecosystem, with grave repercussions for global climate.[12]

Forests, wetlands, and grasslands fulfil vital functions for local climates and water supplies. Their destruction and conversion to farmland are among the largest sources of carbon dioxide emissions.[13] Furthermore, the resulting habitat destruction endangers plant and animal wildlife, compounding the pressure on biodiversity and ecosystems.

Thus, animal agriculture has a doubly damaging effect on climate: not only does it produce huge amounts of harmful greenhouse gas emissions, it also destroys Earth's natural defense systems.

Loss of Fertile Land Diminishes Harvests

Additionally, fertile topsoils such as humus and peat, which are rich in organic matter, are at risk of erosion due to deforestation, wetland drainage, and unsustainable land management. These priceless natural resources cannot be restored within our lifetime. Agricultural machinery, over-fertilisation, toxins, and monocultures deplete and loosen the soil, which is then carried away by wind and rain. Poor soil leads to weak harvests, which in turn necessitate the cultivation of ever-expanding areas of farmland. The earth's soils also act as huge carbon sinks and contain more carbon than the entire atmosphere or all of the planet's vegetation.[14, 15] The destruction of topsoils further compounds the problem of global warming.

Our Food Choices Determines Our Carbon Footprint

Rising incomes and urbanisation across developing countries are driving an increase in meat consumption. These changing demographics are bringing about a global food transition in which less-processed, highly plant-based traditional diets are being replaced by diets higher in refined sugars, refined fats, and animal products. If the consumption of meat and other animal products increases at current rates, global greenhouse gas emissions from animal agriculture will rise by nearly 80% by 2050,[16, 17, 18] making the climate targets set in the Paris Climate Agreement unrealistic. Therefore, reducing animal consumption is a crucial step towards meeting the 2°C target.[19, 20]

Even though consumption of animal products plays a major role in climate change, there is little public awareness of the link between diet and climate change. Recognising the climate impact of different foods is a crucial first step in making climate-friendly food choices.

A Plant-Based Diet Is Climate-Friendly

There is consistent evidence that diets high in plant-based foods and lower in animal products are less damaging to the climate. Consider, for example, that, depending on various factors, producing 1 kg of beef releases between 10 and 30 kg of carbon dioxide into the environment,[21, 22, 23, 24, 25, 26] while producing 1 kg of tofu releases only 1 kg of carbon dioxide.[27] Replacing beef with beans would free up

42% of US farmland, achieve 75% of the US's 2020 climate goal, and provide more than sufficient dietary protein.[28] Studies suggest that personal food-related carbon footprints could be halved with the adoption of a plant-based diet,[29, 30] and that if everyone adopted a vegan diet, worldwide food-related greenhouse gas emissions could be reduced by up to 70% by 2050.[31] Given that, calorie for calorie, meat, dairy, and other animal-based foods create more greenhouse gases and require significantly more land and other resources than plant-based foods, it is easy to conclude that, besides its many other benefits, a plant-based diet is one of the simplest and most effective ways that each one of us can make a positive impact on climate change.

ProVeg Helps Reduce Greenhouse Gasses

ProVeg raises awareness about the climate impact of our food choices by communicating with political decision-makers and civil society organisations. Politicians need to introduce and prioritise food consumption and production, particularly animal agriculture, on both the global climate protection agenda and within national implementation plans. In order to have our voice heard, we team up with others, for example the German Climate Alliance, a strong network of over 100 organisations. Additionally, ProVeg actively negotiates and contributes to national climate change policies through public participation processes.

ProVeg Participates in the World Climate Change Conference (COP)

At COP23 in Bonn, Germany, ProVeg handed over a petition to German State Secretary Jochen Flasbarth, calling for animal agriculture to be put on the agenda. ProVeg also hosted a successful side event with leading scientists, including Marco Springmann from Oxford University and Alon Shepon from the Weizmann Institute of Science.

2018 will be an important climate policy year in which ProVeg will continue to work intensively on the topic and pursue political dialogue in a targeted manner. In Germany, the first package of measures to shape the German climate protection plan, including concrete instruments, is being negotiated. At the international level, the year begins with the so-called Intersessional Conference, during which guidelines and concrete points will be negotiated and prepared for the next Climate Change Conference in Katowice (Poland) (COP24).

References

1, 3. Vermeulen, S. J. et al. (2012): Climate Change and Food Systems. Annual Review of Environment and Resources 37, p.195–222

2. Herrero, M., B. Henderson, P. Havlík, et al. (2016): Greenhouse gas mitigation potentials in the livestock sector. Nature Clim. Change. 6, p.452–461

4. Bajželj, B., J. M. Allwood & J. M. Cullen (2013): Designing Climate Change Mitigation Plans That Add Up. Environ Sci Technol. 47, p.8062–8069

5. Heinrich Böll Stiftung, GRAIN & Institute for Agriculture & Trade Policy (2017): Big Meat and Dairy's supersized Climate Footprint. Available at https://www.grain.org/article/entries/5825-big-meat-and-dairy-s-supersized-climate-footprint [03.03.2018]

6, 9, 10. Gerber, P. et al. (2013): Tackling climate change through livestock: a global assessment of emissions and mitigation opportunities. FAO, Rome. p. 15

7. Myhre, G., D. Shindell, F.-M. Bréon, et al. (2013): Anthropogenic and Natural Radiative Forcing. In: Climate Change 2013: The Physical Science Basis. Contribution of Working Group I to the Fifth Assessment Report of the Intergovernmental Panel on Climate Change [Stocker, T.F., D. Qin, G.-K. Plattner, M. Tignor, S.K. Allen, J. Boschung, A. Nauels, Y. Xia, V. Bex and P.M. Midgley (eds.)]. Cambridge University Press, Cambridge, United Kingdom and New York, NY, USA.

8. Gerber, P. et al. (2013): Tackling climate change through livestock: a global assessment of emissions and mitigation opportunities. FAO, Rome. p.15

11. BBC (2005): Amazon destruction accelerating. Available at http://news.bbc.co.uk/2/hi/americas/4561189.stm [03.03.2018]

12. Saatchi, S., S. Asefi-Najafabady, Y. Malhi,et al (2013): Persistent Effects of a Severe Drought on Amazonian Forest Canopy. Proceedings of the National Academy of Sciences 110, no. 2 (January 8, 2013): 565–570.

13. IPCC (2007): Climate Change 2007: Synthesis Report. Contribution of Working Groups I, II and III to the Fourth Assessment Report of the Intergovernmental Panel on Climate Change [Core Writing Team, Pachauri, R.K and Reisinger, A. (eds.)]. IPCC, Geneva, Switzerland

14. Gobin, A., P. Campling et al. (2011): Soil organic matter management across the EU – best practices, constraints and trade-offs, Final Report for the European Commission's DG Environment, September 2011.

15. Heinrich-Böll-Stiftung, Institute for Advanced Sustainability Studies, and Bund für Umwelt- und Naturschutz Deutschland (2015): Bodenatlas 2015: Daten und Fakten über Acker, Land und Erde.

16. Popp, A. et al. (2010): Food consumption, diet shifts and associated non-CO2 greenhouse gases from agricultural production. Global Environmental Change 20, p.451–462

17. Tilman, D. & M. Clark (2014): Global diets link environmental sustainability and human health. Nature 515, p.518–522

18. Springmann, M. et al. (2016): Analysis and valuation of the health and climate change cobenefits of dietary change. PNAS 113, p.4146–4151

19. Brent Kim et al. (2015): The Importance of Reducing Animal Product Consumption and Wasted Food in Mitigating Catastrophic Climate Change. John Hopkins Center for a Livable Future

20. Hedenus, F., S. Wirsenius & D. J. A. Johansson (2014): The importance of reduced meat and dairy consumption for meeting stringent climate change targets. Climatic Change. 124, p.79–91

21. Vergé, X. P. C., J. A. Dyer, R. L. Desjardins, et al. (2008): Greenhouse gas emissions from the Canadian beef industry. Agricultural Systems. 98, p.126–134

22. Lesschen, J P., M. van der Berg et al. (2011): Greenhouse gas emission profiles of European livestock sectors. Animal Feed Science and Technology, pp. 166-167 and pp. 16-28.

23. Garnett, T. (2009): Livestock-related greenhouse gas emissions: Impacts and options for policy makers. Environmental Science and Policy 12, pp. 491–504.

24. Carlsson-Kanyama, A., & A. D. González (2009): Potential contributions of food consumption patterns to climate change. The American Journal of Clinical Nutrition 2009; 89 (suppl), pp. 1704S-9S.

25. Reinhardt, G., S. Gärtner, Münch, J. & S. Häfele (2009): Ökologische Optimierung regional erzeugter Lebensmittel: Energie- und Klimabilanzen, Heidelberg: IFEU.

26. Venkat, K. (2012): The climate change and economic impacts of food waste in the United States, Portland, OR: CleanMetrics Corp.

27. Mejia, A. et al. (2017): Greenhouse Gas Emissions Generated by Tofu Production: A Case Study. Journal of Hunger & Environmental Nutrition

28. Harwatt, H. et al. (2017): Substituting beans for beef as a contribution toward US climate change targets. Climatic Change doi:10.1007/s10584-017-1969-1

29. Wissenschaftlicher Beirat für Agrarpolitik, Ernährung und gesundheitlichen Verbraucherschutz & Wissenschaftlicher Beirat Waldpolitik beim BMEL (2016): Klimaschutz in der Land- und Forstwirtschaft sowie den nachgelagerten Bereichen Ernährung und Holzverwendung.

30, 31. Scarborough, P. et al. (2014): Dietary greenhouse gas emissions of meat-eaters, fish-eaters, vegetarians and vegans in the UK. Climatic Change 125, p.179–192

Agriculture Is a Major Source of Greenhouse Gas Emissions

Pierce Nahigyan

Pierce Nahigyan is a journalist and editor in chief at Planet Experts.

How much does agricultural activity contribute to greenhouse gas emissions? It's an important question, but one whose answer varies depending on the source. In the U.S., for example, the Environmental Protection Agency has calculated that 5.8 percent of total gross anthropogenic (man-made) emissions of carbon dioxide (CO_2) are associated with the agricultural sector. But that is just one greenhouse gas (GHG) in one nation. Estimates for the total contribution of GHG from all agricultural activities on the planet can reach as high as 51 percent. But is that possible?

A review of the leading scientific literature on the subject suggests that the 51 percent figure is overblown. Instead, analyses by the World Resources Institute (WRI) and the UN Food and Agricultural Organization (UN FAO) place the estimate between 14 and 18 percent of all anthropogenic GHG emissions.

That's significantly less than half of global GHG emissions, yet even the lowest estimate (14 percent) is still neck and neck with WRI's estimated emissions for the transportation sector (13.5 percent). So the question then becomes, *why* does agriculture emit so much GHG?

It's Mostly the Livestock

First, a quick refresher on global warming and greenhouse gases.

The main contributor to global warming is carbon dioxide. While CO_2 nourishes plants and is good for soil, too much of it in the atmosphere is bad for the planet as a whole. CO_2 absorbs the thermal energy of the sun and does not dissipate for a very

"How Much Does Agriculture Contribute to Global Warming?" by Pierce Nahigyan, Planet Experts, LLC, February 9, 2016. Reprinted by permission.

long time, trapping heat very much like a greenhouse does (hence, "greenhouse gas effect"). But CO_2 is not the only greenhouse gas to worry about. The next two most common GHG are methane (CH_4) and nitrous oxide (N_2O). Together, these gases plus CO_2 make up about 99 percent of all GHG in the atmosphere.

While the majority of global warming activities give off carbon dioxide, the agricultural sector primarily emits CH_4 and N_2O. Livestock such as cattle produce methane as part of their digestion cycle. In fact, the CH_4 produced from "enteric fermentation" (i.e., cows farting) represents almost one-third of the emissions from the U.S. agricultural sector, according to the EPA.

Cows are different from pigs and chickens in this regard, as the latter animals do not produce methane. Cows are also significantly more costly to feed and more damaging to the environment. One 2014 study estimates that producing beef requires 28 times more land, six times more fertilizer and 11 times more water than producing pork or chicken. As Skeptical Science explains, this means that "producing beef releases *four times more greenhouse gases* than a calorie-equivalent amount of pork, and five times as much as an equivalent amount of poultry [emphasis added]."

This explains why a very vocal segment of environmentalists insist that eating red meat is bad for the environment and encourage consumers to go vegan. And while it is true that eating too much red meat is bad for your health and a vegan diet is likely the healthiest option (click the links to learn more on these topics), the breakdown of global GHG emissions shows that this claim, too, is somewhat overblown. However, as more developing countries acquire a taste for red meat, cattle production is expected to increase and, with it, GHG emissions.

That's why cutting down on red meat is not the crackpot notion it is frequently painted to be.

Agriculture's GHG emissions do not come from cattle alone. Various methods of irrigation, tillage and soil management lead to the production of N_2O, and the use of manure contributes to both CH_4 and N_2O emissions. Clearing space for agriculture (e.g., deforestation) is also a contributor to carbon emissions and land degradation.

And as the World Future Council points out, soil erosion caused by agriculture and natural processes is also a significant cause for ecological concern. Though not directly related to global warming, its impact will be felt more acutely as the climate changes and the amount of top soil is reduced worldwide.

So What To Do?

Agriculture is arguably the most essential sector of the global economy, but there is something you can do to reduce its GHG emissions at the individual level. As mentioned above, cutting your intake of red meat is a good place to start. Eating more vegetables is a good next step. Again, to quote Skeptical Science:

> "Eating vegetables produces lower greenhouse gas emissions… For example, potatoes, rice, and broccoli produce approximately 3–5 times lower emissions than an equivalent mass of poultry and pork (Environmental Working Group 2011). The reason is simple—it's more efficient to grow a crop and eat it than to grow a crop, feed it to an animal as it builds up muscle mass, then eat the animal."

The most important thing to remember is that global warming is a *global* problem, and improvements are needed in every sector of the economy. Agriculture is not the only emitter of CO_2, N_2O and CH_4, and there are plenty of ways to reduce your global footprint in your daily life. If we all do what we can to use less, recycle more and pursue energy efficient or even net-zero policies, then we can all still have a steak once in a while.

Organizations to Contact

The editors have compiled the following list of organizations concerned with the issues debated in this book. The descriptions are derived from materials provided by the organizations. All have publications or information available for interested readers. This list was compiled on the date of publication of the present volume; the information provided here may change. Be aware that many organizations take several weeks or longer to respond to inquiries, so allow as much time as possible.

Food and Agriculture Organization of the United Nations (FAO)
Viale delle Terme di Caracalla
00153 Rome
Italy
phone: (+39) 06 57051
email: FAO-HQ@fao.org
website: www.fao.org/home/en/

The Food and Agriculture Organization of the United Nations is a globally focused organization dedicated to eradicating world hunger and food insecurity. FAO has over 194 member states working in over 130 countries around the world to make sure that people have access to high quality food that will help them lead healthy lives. This site provides a wealth of information about the topic of global hunger and food insecurity.

Food Tank
phone: (202) 590-1037
email: danielle@foodtank.com
website: www.foodtank.com

Food Tank is a nonprofit organization dedicated to building and educating an online global community that is knowledgeable about safe and healthy food. Read news articles and listen to podcasts about issues of sustainable agriculture.

4-H
7100 Connecticut Avenue
Chevy Chase, MD 20815
phone: (301) 961-2800
website: www.4-h.org

4-H is an organization with local chapters spread across the United States. They inspire kids to grow, learn, and become leaders in agriculture, STEM, healthy living, and civics. Their website has lots of information in these areas, as well as how to find a local group to join or participate in an online STEM lab.

Friends of the Earth
139 Clapham Road
London, SW9 OHP
United Kingdom
phone: (020) 7490 1555
website: www.friendsoftheearth.uk

Friends of the Earth is a worldwide environmental organization. It is based in the UK, but has members spanning seventy-five countries worldwide. This organization encourages members to be active in their local communities with climate change, pollution, and recycling.

Global Citizen
594 Broadway, Suite 207
New York, NY 10012
email: contact@globalcitizen.org
website: www.globalcitizen.org/en/

Global Citizen is an online community made up of members from around the world. This group is dedicated to social issues of today, and one of their main focuses is to end extreme poverty. Read informative articles about a variety of topics aimed at promoting a common, global good.

International Federation of Organic Agriculture Movements (IFOAM)

Charles-de-Gaulle-Str. 5
53113 Bonn
Germany
phone: +49 (0) 228 926 50-10
email: headoffice@ifoam.org
website: www.ifoam.bio/en

International Federation of Organic Agriculture Movements is a globally reaching organization with members in over 127 countries. The organization advocates for sustainable production using organic agriculture and consumer awareness. IFOAM maintains an online library and blog to spread the word about organic farming.

National FFA Association (FFA)

6060 FFA Drive
Indianapolis, IN 46268-0960
phone: (888) 332-2668
website: www.ffa.org

The National FFA Association—or Future Farmers of America—is an organization dedicated to providing young people with the tools to become leaders in the field of agriculture. The FFA aims to prepare not only the future generation of farmers, but also biologists, chemists, veterinarians, engineers, entrepreneurs, and more. Read and learn all about other young people active in the broad area of agriculture.

Organic Farmers Association (OFA)
611 Siegfriedale Road
Kutztown, PA 19530-9320
phone: (610) 683-1475
email: OFA@RodaleInstitute.org
website: www.organicfarmersassociation.org

The Organic Farmers Association launched in 2016 as a group of organic farmers wanting to join together for a better future. This nonprofit group is dedicated to research and outreach to make organic farming work for the farmers and benefit consumers. Watch webinars on issues of importance to organic farming.

United States Department of Agriculture (USDA)
1400 Independence Avenue SW
Washington, DC 20250
phone: (202) 720-2791
email: askusda@usda.gov
website: www.usda.gov

The US Department of Agriculture is a governmental organization comprised of twenty-nine different agencies. This agency was started by President Abraham Lincoln and is dedicated to providing leadership in many areas, including agriculture, natural resources, conservation, and others. Find information about animals, biotechnology, organic farming, and more on the organization's website.

World Hunger Education Service (WHES)
PO Box 29015
Washington, DC 20017
phone: (202) 579-0849
email: info@worldhunger.org
website: www.worldhunger.org

The World Hunger Education Service was founded in 1976 with the purpose of educating the public about hunger and malnutrition across the United States and around the world. WHES maintains a website, Hunger Notes, which provides communication and information about current issues surrounding hunger.

World Resources Institute (WRI)
10 G Street NE, Suite 800
Washington, DC 20002
phone: (202) 729-7600
website: www.wri.org

World Resources Institute is an organization that promotes inclusion, equity, and diversity in a global workforce. The agency is dedicated to protecting Earth's environment and to provide for the needs of current and future generations. WRI focuses on seven global challenges to meet its goals of reducing poverty, protecting natural systems, and growing economies.

Bibliography

Books

Stephanie Anderson. *One Size Fits None: A Farm Girl's Search for the Promise of Regenerative Agriculture*. Lincoln, NE: University of Nebraska Press, 2019.

Michael Brown. *Eating Dangerously: Why the Government Can't Keep Your Food Safe...and How You Can*. Louisville, CO: Rowman & Littlefield Publishers, 2014.

Nancy F. Castaldo. *The Story of Seeds: From Mendel's Garden to Your Plate, and How's There's More of Less to Eat Around the World*. New York, NY: Houghton Mifflin Harcourt, 2016.

Jennifer Culp. *Using Computer Science in Agribusiness*. New York, NY: Rosen Publishing, 2019.

Peter V. Fossel. *Organic Farming: How to Raise, Certify, and Market Organic Crops and Livestock*. McGregor, MN: Voyageur Press, 2014.

Ted Genoways. *This Blessed Earth: A Year in the Life of an American Family Farm*. New York, NY: W. W. Norton & Company, 2017.

Richard Horan. *Harvest: An Adventure into the Heart of America's Family Farms*. New York, NY: Harper Perennial, 2012.

McKay Jenkins. *Food Fight: GMOs and the Future of the American Diet*. New York, NY: Penguin, 2017.

Amanda Little. *The Fate of Food: What We'll Eat in a Bigger, Hotter, Smarter World*. New York, NY: Harmony, 2019.

Christy Mihaly. *Diet for a Changing Climate: Food for Thought*. Minneapolis, MN: 21st Century Books, 2019.

Paul A. Offit. *Pandora's Lab: Seven Stories of Science Gone Wrong*. New York, NY: National Geographic Partners, LLC, 2017.

Robin O'Sullivan. *American Organic: A Cultural History of Farming, Gardening, Shopping and Eating*. Lawrence, KS: University of Kansas Press, 2015.

Caitlyn Shetterly. *Modified: GMOs and the Threat to Our Food, Our Land, Our Future*. New York, NY: G. P. Putnam's Sons, 2016.

Melanie Warner. *Pandora's Lunchbox: How Processed Food Took Over the American Meal*. New York, NY: Scribner, 2013.

Rosamund Young. *The Secret Life of Cows*. New York, NY: Penguin Press, 2018.

Periodicals and Internet Sources

David Biello, "Will Organic Food Fail to Feed the World?" *Scientific American*, April 25, 2012. www.scientificamerican.com/article/organic-farming-yields-and-feeding-the-world-under-climate-change/.

Matty Byloos, "5 Important Elements of Sustainable Agriculture," *Planet Matters*, July 20, 2011. planetmattersandmore.com/sustainable-agriculture-2/five-important-elements-of-sustainable-agriculture/.

Damian Carrington, "UN Experts Denounce 'Myth' Pesticides are Necessary to Feed the World," *Guardian*, March 7, 2017. www.theguardian.com/environment/2017/mar/07/un-experts-denounce-myth-pesticides-are-necessary-to-feed-the-world.

Steven Druker, "The UK's Royal Society: A Case Study in How the Health Risk of GMO's Have Been Systematically Misrepresented," *Independent Science News*, August 14, 2017. www.independentsciencenews.org/health/the-uks

-royal-society-how-the-health-risks-of-gmos-have-been
-systematically-misrepresented/.

Susie Fagan, "Big Money, the Farm Bill and Family Farms Vs.
Industrial Agriculture," *American Promise*, June 18, 2019.
www.americanpromise.net/big-money-the-farm-bill-and
-family-farms-vs-industrial-agriculture/.

Alicia Harvie, "What is a Family Farm? How Does if Differ
from a Factory Farm?" Farm Aid, April 9, 2010. www
.farmaid.org/issues/industrial-agriculture/what-exactly-is
-a-family-farm/.

Tamar Haspel, "Small vs. Large: Which Size Farm is Better for
the Planet?" *Washington Post*, September 2, 2014. www
.washingtonpost.com/lifestyle/food/small-vs-large-which
-size-farm-is-better-for-the-planet/2014/08/29/ac2a3dc8
-2e2d-11e4-994d-202962a9150c_story.html.

Jillian Kubala, "What Is the Impossible Burger, and Is It
Healthy?" EcoWatch, April 27, 2019. www
.ecowatch.com/impossible-burger-2635663466
.html?rebelltitem=1#rebelltitem1

James M. MacDonald, "Large Family Farms Continue to
Dominate U.S. Agricultural Production," US Department of
Agriculture, March 6, 2017. www.ers.usda.gov/amber
-waves/2017/march/large-family-farms-continue-to
-dominate-us-agricultural-production/.

Stacy Malkan, "GMO's. 2.0—The Truth About the Next Wave
of Genetically Modified Foods," *Food Revolution Network*,
April 4, 2018. http://foodrevolution.org/blog/new
-genetically-modified-food/.

Joseph Mercola, "Fake Meat is Junk Food," *MERCOLA*,
September 25, 2019. http://articles.mercola.com/sites
/articles/archive/2019/09/25/fake-meat-is-junk-food.aspx.

Lauran Neergaard, "Next Generation of Biotech Food Heading for Grocery Shelves," *WSAZ News*, November 14, 2018. www.wsaz.com/content/news/Gene-edited-food-is-coming -but-will-shoppers-buy-500495161.html.

Jean Nick, "But Can Organic Farming Feed the World?" Nature's Path, May 26, 2017. www.naturespath.com/en-us /blog/but-can-organic-farming-feed-the-world/.

Christina Nunez, "What's Better for the World: Local Farms or Large Agribusiness?" *Global Citizen*, February 16, 2015. www.globalcitizen.org/en/content/whats-better-for-the -world-local-farms-or-large-ag/.

Gracy Olmstead, "Down on the Farm," *National Review,* August 15, 2016. www.nationalreview.com/2016/08/small-farms -big-business-family-farms-struggle-against-industrial -agriculture/.

Monica Reinagel, "Meet GenED: The Next Generation of Biotechnology," *Food & Nutrition*, March 1, 2018. https:// foodandnutrition.org/from-the-magazine/meet-gened -next-generation-biotechnology/.

Index